SOUL TRIBES AND TAMBOS

Communities for Souls on the Move

John P. Davidson

Copyright © 2014 John P. Davidson.

All rights reserved. No part of this book may be used or reproduced in any manner without written permission from the author.

HeartWorks Publishing is a trademark of HeartWorks Publishing Company

Cover Photo: John P. Davidson
Cover art and design: Charlotte Hollis
Interior Book Design: Booknook.biz

Davidson, John P. (John Philip)
   Soul tribes and tambos: communities for souls on the move / John P. Davidson.

      pages cm
      ISBN 978-0-9882557-4-6

    1. Soul. 2. Spirituality. 3. Peru--Religion.
    4. Ayahuasca. 5. Ethnobotany.   I. Title.
BL290.D38 2014   128'.1
                      QBI14-600022

ISBN 978-0-9882557-4-6
Library of Congress Control Number: 2014902301

HeartWorks Publishing Company
P.O. Box 6
Raton, New Mexico 87740
USA
www.heartworkspublishing.com

OTHER BOOKS BY JOHN P. DAVIDSON

The Soul's Critical Path: Waking Down to the Soul's Purpose, the Body's Power, and the Heart's Passion

The Left Hand of God: A Soul's Love Poems

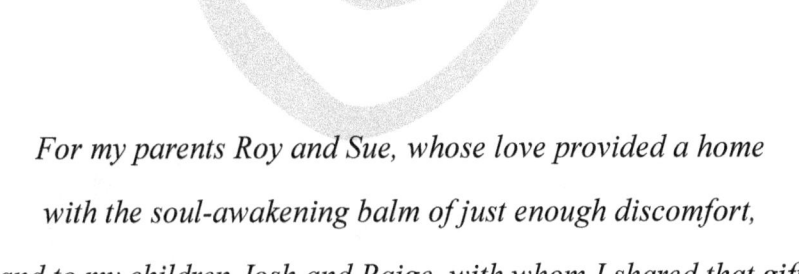

For my parents Roy and Sue, whose love provided a home with the soul-awakening balm of just enough discomfort, and to my children Josh and Paige, with whom I shared that gift

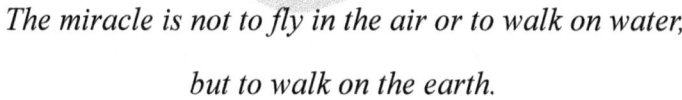

The miracle is not to fly in the air or to walk on water,

but to walk on the earth.

CHINESE PROVERB

CONTENTS

AUTHOR'S FOREWORD	xi
PROLOGUE	xiii
PREFACE	xv
INTRODUCTION	xix
CHAPTER 1	
CHASKIS, TAMBOS, AND THE NEW INVASION OF PERU	1
CHAPTER 2	
SIX STORIES	23
Zera	23
Grace	24
Sarah	26
Jane	29
Robin	33
CHAPTER 3	
MANY TRIBES	39
CHAPTER 4	
STAGES OF TRIBAL CONSCIOUSNESS	47
Stage One	49
Stage Two	49
Stage Three	51
Stage Four	54
Stage Five	55
CHAPTER 5	
SLEEPING SOULS, SLEEPING TRIBES	57
Sleeping Souls	57
Sleeping Tribes	60
CHAPTER 6	
CHOOSING WHERE THE SOUL WILL WORK	69

CHAPTER 7
>	PLANT SHAMANS AND PACOS: COMPLEMENTARY
>	TRADITIONS 75

CHAPTER 8
>	THE Q'ERO PACOS: OUR SOULS ARE SOLAR 83

CHAPTER 9
>	THE ENTHEOGENIC PLANTS 87
>	>	Ayahuasca 91
>	>	Huachuma 96
>	>	Thoughts of Collaboration 102

CHAPTER 10
>	SOUL TRIBES AND TAMBOS 109
>	>	A Support Community with a Soul Perspective 109
>	>	The Prime Process Objective 110
>	>	Elders 113
>	>	The Agreement 113
>	>	A Curriculum 114
>	>	Place 116
>	>	Right Relationship with Place 118
>	>	Ceremony and Prayer 119
>	>	Awe-Ful Science 122
>	>	A Collaborative Team 124
>	>	The Plants 126
>	>	Food 127
>	>	Research 128
>	>	Balancing Specialization with Generalization 129
>	>	Grounding 130

CHAPTER 11
>	A SOUL HOME OF THE HEART 131

AN AFTERWORD FROM GRACE   133

APPENDIX   139

AUTHOR'S FOREWORD

THIS BOOK IS A COMPANION to my first book, The Soul's Critical Path: Waking Down to the Soul's Purpose, the Body's Power, and the Heart's Passion. That book provides a soul-eye view of our journey to earth, the soul's gradual remembrance of who it is, and the work that precedes the soul's ultimate partnering with its first and most important soul mate, which is the body. I described in that book four distinct stages through which the soul must travel before it can fully mate the body to begin the fifth stage. That last stage is the process of co-creating the world in this dense dimension of matter.

In this book I have undertaken to describe a model for small communities that support the increasingly awake and mobile souls that are traveling the planet in search of themselves, their passions, and each other. I have attempted to make this book stand on its own so that it is not necessary to read the first to make sense of this one. However, if you resonate with the message of this book, I would suggest your reading that first book for the more detailed exposition of the construct that supports this book. To make the connection between the two books a little easier, I have attached an appendix to this book that represents a summary of the central message of that first book.

The names of the women whose interviews appear in Chapter Two have been changed except in those cases where permission was given to use actual names.

PROLOGUE

Where are the *chakaruna,*
the old ones
who know,
who know who they are
and why we are here?
Where are they,
the ones who bridge,
who bridge heaven to earth,
whose hearts
center the universe?

Don't look on the mountain,
in the forest
or the jungle,
across the great river
or behind ashram walls.
The forests are floating
in the rivers,
the mountains mined,
our hearts escaping
only by benign neglect.

The old ones are back
disguised in young faces,
fresh from heaven
with tablets glowing
in their hands.
They are awakening
to who they are,
still shaking off
fate's enforced forgetting
felt like jet lag
multiplied by millennia,
their commandments writ large
on souls still smoking,
their eyes burning
with heaven's fire
and coffee.

They are in the airports,
moving fast and wide,
feeling the planet,
taking stock,
triaging the carnage,
trying to remember
who they *really* are,
what their work is *this* time
while things heat up
and humanity teeters.

I say
walk with them,
wake them quickly,
tell them the one thing
they need to know.
I say
show them *how* to know,
how to listen with their *hearts*
so they will know again
who they are,
why we are here
and what they have to do.

PREFACE

AT CRITICAL TIMES throughout human history, relatively more evolved soul groups gather on the planet. They come to help.

Such souls are known by many names throughout the world. In the traditional Quechua language of Peru, these souls are known as the *chakaruna*. They are little seen, and their work is little understood.

The chakaruna are bridges. They bridge between our dimension and the other-dimensional fields of intelligence that seek to support the evolution of human consciousness in service of the evolution of consciousness itself.

That process of evolution supports creation, a process so shrouded in mystery that human minds cannot fully understand it, even as we know it intimately. We know it because we are an inherent part of that process. Fully conscious or not, humans are the engine of creation. And creation proceeds one soul at a time.

The knowledge base that accumulates from this soul work is itself continuously evolving. That knowledge accumulates from the interaction between earth-based souls and the myriad other-dimensional fields of intelligence that inhabit what we often call "heaven" or "cosmos" and "earth." The knowledge is about heaven's relationship with matter—how heaven's design manifests in the realm of matter.

Humans are the connection between these other-dimensional intelligences and the living matter—*mater*—we know as earth. The earth mother rises up to receive this design information and collaborate in the process of creation when humans can meet her in full awareness of their role. Those humans who meet the earth in full awareness of their role are the chakaruna.

The chakaruna have reincarnated over time in order to *receive, embody, protect, evolve, record,* and *translate* the processes by which human souls co-evolve with the planetary soul in service of creation. Each of these six tasks is a separate and distinct piece of work. Successive soul lifetimes are devoted to such work.

The earth soul and the collective of human souls have reached an obvious and critical juncture in their relatively young relationship. The United States' fragile two-and-a-half-century experiment with democracy and capitalism has run into a perfect storm of resistance, ironically and primarily homegrown. That resistance comes in the form of corporate domination of the political process, now more powerful and numerous than the corporations that pre-existed the bubble of prosperity that arose in the United States in the latter part of the twentieth century.

With the profits of that prosperity, multinational corporations have purchased control of the United States government and much of the process of scientific research. Politicians across the political spectrum have sold their public offices to these corporations at remarkably low prices. These corporations operate under cover of the pseudo-science of neoclassical economics and the mantra of free markets. They control the flow of information with a bought-and-paid-for media using increasingly sophisticated technology. In this way, these corporations have captured the culture of the United States and are now destroying the middle class upon which democracy depends.

The immorality of corporations has converged with the amorality of science and technology and with the human propensity for short-term thinking. This convergence, in combination with unsustainable levels of human population, is destroying the environment upon which planetary life depends and is bringing humanity to the brink of devastation. We cannot predict how far and fast the fall will be. But we can predict with some confidence that it will occur, and relatively sooner than later.

In response to this challenge, the chakaruna are gathering in greater numbers on the planet. Some of the chakaruna will work within developed but deeply unconscious cultures in an attempt to reverse what now appears inevitable, or to soften its consequences. Some will work to speed the fall of these corporate power structures. Others will work in less developed but more earth-connected cultures to minimize the ongoing damage and turn them from following developed countries over the edge. Some of these souls will focus upon bringing compassionate means to diminish the already deep suffering that will increase exponentially as humans move into this next phase of human experience. Others will work to create sustainable solutions to the challenge of living on the planet. Yet other souls may be on the planet to focus on personal work best done during times of great challenge.

And all of these souls will need support.

Sometimes, when these old souls reside in younger humans, they need to be reminded that they are souls with significant gifts and responsibilities equal to the measure of those gifts. They need to be reminded that they have been here before and that they are here again to do the work of personal and planetary destiny. They need help in learning how their special gifts can be grounded and get traction on the planet. They need help to assess the times into which they have been born. Sometimes they need to know where others of their kind are gathering to do the work. All of these souls are more citizens of the world than of any one of the fading nation-states, and they tend to be mobile.

They are all of one tribe. They need a place that provides the support this soul tribe needs—a place they might call *home.*

Soul Tribes and Tambos suggests a new kind of home for these shining souls, one that is dedicated to supporting soul evolution in an accelerating time domain.

INTRODUCTION

NO SENSE IS MORE CENTRAL to the human psyche than the notion of home. Yet throughout human history, humans have left their homes. Some left because they chose to, some because they had to. Some were pulled, and some were pushed.

For many, the memory of their birth home rests ever softly in their hearts and calls them back, or calls them forward to discover another such home. For others, the painfully mandatory memory of home carries the wound that chased and then followed them into the larger world.

So many of us have forgotten what many pre-modern cultures believed—that the psyche is itself the soul, and that the body and earth are the temporary home of souls that have chosen to journey away from an other-dimensional home. Just as humans migrate from their homes, souls have migrated from their home in heaven. Heaven is a name we have given to a mystery to which we know ourselves to be connected but do not understand. Not remembering who we are, neither can we remember where we came from.

Just as the soul has separated from its heavenly home, so has the physical body separated from its earthly home. The body's energetic umbilical cord has been severed from the earth Mother, an experience perhaps more deeply felt in the cultures like the

United States that have separated themselves from the daily relationship with the earth that came with subsistence farming.

Home calls still to souls and bodies alike. Like a persistent flame of hope, the call of home burns in our bodies and souls, and we know it most deeply in our hearts.

During the time that the idea for this book was just a tickle in my consciousness, I found myself in the midst of my own search for home. I had followed my heart to Peru as my connection to my relatively more comfortable home in the United States waned. The recovery of a sense of home would have to await the heart's work of zeroing in on some place in particular as the future unfolded. In the meantime, and without a place to call home, I found my notion of home beginning to morph. For the time, at least, I found home in my relationship with my traveling companion Darlene Joy, and in my own heart, regardless of where I might lay my head for the night. But I never felt complete in the sense of a connection with place. Some place beyond the horizon of my ability to see forward continued to call.

I was not alone in this search, of course. In Peru, I found many travelers searching for a sense of connection they associated with a place called home. Many of these were young people who had left their homes with no strong desire to return. Each expressed, in some way, a desire for a place they could rest and settle, at least for a time. They wanted a home that resonated with their own sense of who they were becoming, even as they knew that they were on a quest that might preclude settling down for some time to come.

There was another theme consistently present in my conversations with these young explorers. Each was responding to a need to discover something within themselves that few of them could articulate. In light of my own soul perspective on the nature of humans, I understood their underlying drive to arise from the soul's need to infuse the less consciousness personality with a passion of soul purpose. In these young people, I saw particularly strong soul impulses they had not yet recognized as such, but to which they had responded by leaving job, home, family, and country to journey in the unfamiliar toward an unknown destination.

The context in which these conversations occurred provided a third theme beyond the notions of soul emergence and the search for home. Our exchanges often occurred around ceremonies with *ayahuasca* and *San Pedro*, two entheogenic plant medicines found in Peru. Darlene and I had come to Peru to drink these plant medicines because of our belief in their capacity to hasten the process of soul emergence. And speed was what we experienced, compared to the results of spiritual and psychological technologies of consciousness with which we had spent considerable time in earlier years. With this sense of speed came another, related sense—a foreshortening of time in general.

For me, this sense of accelerating time came most intensely in ceremonies I experienced in the month of December, 2012. As I listened during those ceremonies, I sensed that the various other-dimensional intelligences that concern themselves with the progress of human souls had begun to push more and more to be heard by awakening human souls. At the same time, I sensed that there were more and more souls on the planet both listening and responding to those same other-dimensional voices.

I sensed a synergy in this exchange. The more we listened to those on the other side, the more they could connect. The more they connected, the more we could hear. The more we could hear and respond, the faster became the communication that underwrites the evolution of consciousness. Souls that are awakening now to the reality that they are souls with a destiny just before them are becoming drivers of this increasing rate of change.

These three themes—soul emergence, the search for home, and the acceleration of the rate of change—were beginning to connect in my thinking. Souls were unfolding in our presence. Characteristic of these souls was a deep desire for a home different from the one they had left, even as they lacked a clear vision of what they yearned for. And time was speeding up around these souls as they pushed off from old shores and swam into the turbulent center of time's river.

In my earlier book, *The Soul's Critical Path,* I described how the adoption of an experiential soul perspective allows the awakening soul to bring the personality and the body into partnership with the soul's agenda for this lifetime, and to do so more quickly than souls have evolved over thousands of lifetimes. I suggested several stages by which the soul transcends its fate and embraces the process of discovering and creating its destiny. Moving through these stages requires that the soul: (1) remember that it is a soul, (2) anchor itself in the field of the heart, (3) learn to navigate using the lens of the heart, (4) create for the body the sense of love and safety that is the condition for the release of wounding held by the body, (5) infuse the personality with the soul's presence in order to develop a partnership between soul and body that gives power and passion to the soul's purpose, and (6) create a collaborative relationship with the density of matter that provides the context in which the soul participates in the co-creation of the universe.

The Soul's Critical Path also suggested the presence of a spiritual paradox that confronts the modern soul. United States culture provides an unprecedented but confusing smorgasbord of spiritual offerings in a setting that encourages soul growth by the very fact of its soul-repressive nature. I suggested that we can dine at this smorgasbord more wisely by fusing the skill of controlling attention with the skill of knowing the multiplicity of places we can put it. Asian meditation cultures have taught us how to control attention, and the indigenous shamanic cultures now offer to teach us to bring that attention to our relationship with the earth. Combining these complementary perspectives, we have a greater opportunity to bring all the resources of heaven and earth to bear on the process of our personal soul evolution for the benefit of the evolution of consciousness as a whole.

Soul Tribes and Tambos takes a next step, addressing the aspect of the soul's journey that occurs of necessity in relationship to community. I have extended the notion of the soul's internal stages of consciousness described in *The Soul's Critical Path* to communities themselves. Souls that are consciously awakening need communities in which soul evolution is purposely and skillfully supported at all levels.

In Peru, I could see some movement toward such communities, but I did not see such communities fully developed. I did not see a community that serves the soul's simultaneous needs for freedom, support, guidance, and skill development in a context of increasingly conscious connection with the earth, plants, and places of power—all in a setting that a soul on the move can experience as home, even if the stay is relatively temporary.

Tambos is the name I have given to the notion of places where a particular *soul tribe* can form the kind of community that provides this special set of supports for the soul in conscious pursuit of its destiny. Souls on the move need many homes where they can experience the love, support, and respite that the notion of home inherently includes.

The vision and idea of soul tribes and tambos arose for me from listening. I listened in ceremony with the plant medicines and in my meditative journeys. I listened to other people speak of what they had heard and seen in their own journeys and why they had come to Peru to participate in these ceremonies. I asked what they wanted and needed to support their soul journeys. Their responses deeply informed this book's message.

Chapter Two relates the stories of six of those people—all young women. Of the men and women to whom I listened, the visions of these particular women were the most clear, best informed my inquiry, and resonated most deeply with the vision that was also emerging in me.

Listening to them, I began to understand that the notion of soul tribes and tambos has not originated with me in any personal sense. It felt instead like a broadcast emanating from fields of intelligence that are available to all of us, arriving in the consciousness of those of us who are both listening and having an interest in communities of this kind. We may experience the broadcast as an idea, or as a vision that wants to be seen, shared, and manifested. The vision is emerging in the consciousness of many who yearn for soul emergence, home, and an expeditious path forward. I found a more complete sense of the idea when I brought all of these conversations together.

While the context for the development of this idea has been the quickly evolving spiritual culture in Peru, the seed of this idea can take root anywhere. It can happen in a place where souls gather in readiness to reclaim their identity from unconscious personalities and do the work of partnering with healed bodies. With this intention, they can begin a more conscious process of co-creating in partnership with heaven and earth.

The earth soul also awaits our souls' full awakening to a new partnership with her. That partnership can emerge when enough humans are able to transcend the mother-child relationship with the earth that has been necessary to bring us to this juncture but no longer serves the forward movement of the evolution of consciousness. Rather than seeing earth simply as our mother, we need to mature into capable and intentional partners with an evolving earth soul. The earth soul now demands more of us than a mother can expect of mere children or rebellious teenagers.

Forward movement now depends on our discovering that we *are* souls, on our souls suffusing our personalities, and on the recognition that we need to create the communities that support our becoming who we have the capacity to be. Creating new homes now will support a new partnership with the earth and support the evolution of those souls who can foster this relationship.

I

CHASKIS, TAMBOS, AND THE NEW INVASION OF PERU

BEFORE IT ENDED ABRUPTLY with the Spanish invasion almost 500 years ago, the brief 125-year reign of the Incan culture established an expansive empire that included parts of modern-day Ecuador, Peru, Colombia, Argentina, Chile, and Bolivia. To manage such an expanse, the Incas needed an effective means of communication. For that purpose, they created tambos, shelters that served as lodging and resting places for official messengers called *chaskis*.

The chaskis were fast young runners, moving from tambo to tambo with messages essential to the empire's governance. Many of these tambos were expanded by the Incas into larger planned settlements, still exemplified by the relatively well-preserved community of Ollantaytambo in southern Peru's Sacred Valley.

Today, new versions of chaskis and tambos are proliferating in Peru. The original chaskis were most probably male. Now, both men and women—many of them young—are moving rapidly across Peru and neighboring South American countries. They are coming from all over the world, and they are networking in person and with technology at a rate the Incas might have envied. For many of them, the journey is of a spiritual nature.

Many of these new chaskis are heading to the Peruvian jungles and the area in and around the ancient Inca capital city of Cusco. In both areas, centers are popping up to serve Peru's burgeoning spiritual tourism. In these centers, there are lodges that are often called tambos.

In the jungle, these tambos are sometimes set above the ground on poles, with floors and half-walls of rough-sawn planks topped by a roof made of leaves. In the higher elevations, the walls may be stone or adobe, and the roofs grass or tile. Like the ancient tambos, these are places of rest. The tambos in which I rested had been updated, however, with composting toilets, beds, and colorful hammocks.

The notion of tambos came to mind as I was looking for a way to describe a still inarticulate idea that was trying to form as I found myself back in the Peruvian jungle near Iquitos in 2012, the third time within a year. The concept related to the work I was developing, which is about providing a program of support to souls working to create their destinies.

In the midst of that reflection, I watched people from North America, South America, Australia, and Europe coming to Peru to drink a bitter medicine known as ayahuasca, despite the inevitable purging, frequent diarrhea, and often intimidating visions and voices that accompany this process.

Drinking ayahuasca is by no means a recreational activity, and it is not a drug in the common usage of that term, despite the fact that it is illegal to use ayahuasca in the United States outside the context of certain sanctioned religious ceremonies. In Peru, the plant medicine is not only legal but regarded as a national treasure.

The only buzz ayahuasca creates is on the Internet. Nothing in my own experience would suggest that it is addictive. None of the symptoms of addiction—craving, withdrawal, denial, lying, sneaking, increasing tolerance, irresponsible or self-destructive behavior, self-sabotage, constricted grief, general numbness, or depression—arise from the engagement with ayahuasca.

The engagement is, however, rigorous. Compared to many whom I watched struggle with their encounters with the ayahuasca,

I have been blessed for the most part with relatively gentle experiences that were for me still very challenging. It is a medicine in the most original sense of that word, which derives from the Latin word *medicus,* meaning *physician.*

The Spanish word ayahuasca is derived from the Quechua words for soul (*aya*) and vine or rope (*huasca).* The Quechua language was and remains the predominant language of the indigenous peoples within much of what was the Incan empire, including some portion of Peru's jungle. The medicine itself is a combination of the jungle vine known by this name and other plants, such as *chakaruna,* that activate the ayahuasca's potential effect.

Much has been written about ayahuasca during the past several decades, particularly its chemical makeup and its psychoactive effects. Yet it remains little understood either by those who have directly experienced it or the biochemists who have analyzed its molecular structure. With direct experience of its effects over time, one can sense its power, learn to hear its voice, and connect with the intelligences that empower it. But none of this equates with an understanding of what the plant truly represents, any more than our experience of God gives rise to a coherent understanding of the infinite intelligence to which we have given that name and thousands more.

Although I had managed to elicit many soul gifts from this plant, I could not help but wonder whether the courageous people I met would be able to find the gift in their rigorous experience and integrate it into their lives. Yet, I didn't question *why* people came. That was apparent from my own earliest experience.

I had come to Peru for the first time in 2000 to drink the ayahuasca. This "vine of the soul" lived up to its name during my first encounter. In the course of five nighttime ceremonies spanning a period of ten days, the plant irrevocably loosened the vise grip by which my analytical mind held my attention despite years of meditation. It turned my attention toward my heart, healed my body's affliction with a number of lifelong allergies, and set the stage for a radical redirection of the trajectory of my life—all work of the soul.

I told the story of these radical changes in *The Soul's Critical Path*. However, as I observed in that earlier book, this tsunami of a plant only opened a door, creating a wave of opportunity that could have bobbed me up dramatically before merely passing me by. I had to learn in my own time that it was up to me to catch that wave. To do so, I had to pull up the anchor of my own prior cultural conditioning and integrate the lessons of that experience. I had to complete the initial healing that the ayahuasca brought to the many psychological woundings my body carried, in order to create the life changes that this extraordinary gift offered.

Only years after my initial experience with ayahuasca could I begin to understand that my fifteen years of meditation practice, including numerous vision quests in nature, were a likely factor in my being able to integrate the initial gifts of my encounter with the plant. I say "initial gifts" because a much deeper relationship with the plant had yet to occur. What followed would inspire and require a deeper and different form of meditation—a heart-centered, soul-based, earth-and-heaven-connected focus of attention within the frame of the body. Finding this attentional tool helped me catch the wave of opportunity in a more powerful way.

The force of that wave pulled me back to Peru in 2002 with an American teacher of shamanism whose program was loosely based in the traditions of the *Q'ero*. The Q'ero are a small group of indigenous Peruvians reputed to have escaped the invading Spaniards by fleeing to an area high upon the slopes of Ausangate, an imposing mountain in southern Peru. Ausangate is among the most powerful of the Andean *apus*—mountain spirits—that figure centrally in the indigenous tradition that preceded and includes the Incan culture. The Q'ero lived in relative isolation upon the shoulders of this mountain spirit for hundreds of years before coming down only three decades or so ago to mingle with a much-changed Peruvian culture.

Anthropologists say that the spiritual practices of the Q'ero more closely approximate those of the Incas than what is otherwise found in Peru. That pronouncement has lent a cachet of mystery and respect to the Q'ero that is only enhanced by their long impoverished and isolated existence. As demand for the teaching of indigenous shamanic practices has spiraled upward in developed countries, the Q'ero have become a primary attraction for spiritual tourists. Now, individuals from the Q'ero Nation and shamans from other Peruvian traditions travel internationally to teach their worldview and techniques for experiencing it.

In my initial visit to Machu Picchu and other Peruvian sites in 2002, I found myself traveling on a chartered bus with several Q'eros who performed ceremonies, healings, and initiations along the way. At every opportunity, they unfolded their blanket backpacks into mini-markets of textiles, bells, stones, and feathers—supplies for would-be shamans at prices much higher than those for which I could buy the same items in any market along the way. And my traveling companions and I bought, feeling the need to support this waning culture and hoping that some magic had rubbed off on our purchases.

I experienced a dramatic healing on that trip. On a night when we made camp near Moray, an archeological site an hour away from Cusco, I entered a small tent where Don Umberto and Dona Bernadina had set up shop to do healings. They were an older Q'ero couple in their seventies. A translator was present and asked what I wanted to have healed. I told her that I suffered from motion sickness, a condition exacerbated by riding in hot buses on winding mountain roads. The translator said that Umberto and Bernadina would not know what motion sickness was, but that it didn't matter.

Umberto and Bernadina proceeded to prepare a *despacho*—a ritualized offering wrapped in gift paper and burned as a prayer to the earth Mother known in Peru as the Pachamama and to the apus. Throughout the hour-long preparation of the despacho, Umberto and Bernadina laughed and played with me, continuously encouraging me to participate in the process of placing coca leaves, candies, flowers, and numerous other small objects onto the paper.

I learned from the translator that they had been married since their teen years. Their joyous nature shone through all that occurred between us. My motion sickness abated for the rest of the trip, and it was several months before it resumed.

Although the Q'ero tradition does not include the use of entheogenic plants, it represents a connection with the cosmos as powerful as that accessed by the plant medicines. In *The Soul's Critical Path,* I describe my experience of a vision of the prospective inner marriage of the feminine and masculine. The vision came during and as a direct result of a Q'ero initiation called the *kawak.* Occurring in 2003, my vision was as powerful as any induced by drinking the ayahuasca. It provided the warp for the ayahuasca's weft, allowing me to begin a long process of weaving my own understanding of the changes that had offered themselves to me in these shamanic encounters. Whatever else the ayahuasca experience brought to me, it was initially about the feminine emerging—in me, in both sexes, in the West, the world, and the cosmos. With the kawak, the Q'ero helped to weave me more directly into the story of that emergence.

To be introduced to these Peruvian traditions through an American teacher of shamanism who represented the Q'ero as a shamanic culture turned out to be both ironic and confusing. In 2013, I spent two days with Don Umberto and Dona Bernadina in the United States. During the course of participating in two different despacho ceremonies and receiving two *karpay* initiations (the transmission of a fifth dimensional frequency), I listened to their American spokesman take pains to say that the Q'ero do not consider themselves shamans, but mystics. The spokesperson's narrative suggested that the Q'ero hold more in common with Tibetan Buddhism than with traditions of shamanism that use rattles, drums, and plant medicines, as do the Amazonian shamans of Peru. The practitioners of the Q'ero spiritual traditions, he said, call themselves *pacos,* an appellation not to be confused with the word "shaman." I'll speak more of the significance of this distinction and its relevance to soul tribes and tambos in Chapter Seven.

After my initial visits to Peru in 2000 and 2002, I returned annually to learn more of shamanism and because I had become fascinated with observing life in a developing country. I discovered that traveling in Peru was helping me to understand what it meant to live in my own very developed country. "The best way to see the United States," I started saying tongue-in-cheek to friends back home, "is to leave it."

What my friends didn't understand and what I could only appreciate in time was that my experience of Peruvian culture, with its indigenous roots still showing, was shaking my own North American tribal perspective. I began to see the presumptuous, dangerously paranoid, neoliberal-capitalistic, arrogant mind-set through which the United States sees and engages the rest of the world.

In contrast to the ubiquitous presence of small-scale family farming in rural Peru, the United States had left family farming behind after World War II. I began to realize that, in doing so, the United States had also abandoned a relationship with the land that had allowed it to feed and sustain itself in a relatively healthier relationship with the earth. I argued in *The Soul's Critical Path* that the increase in disease epidemics and psychological distress affecting both children and adults stems in significant part from this single development in our recent history.

In Peru, I saw that the Peruvian *campesinos* still knew how to grow food without chemical fertilizers and pesticides, even as I saw that global corporations were working diligently to cure that ignorance. As of 2013, Peru has seen fit to bar genetically modified seeds from entering the country.

In 2004, I briefly revisited the ayahuasca and encountered San Pedro (*huachuma* in Quechua), the other plant medicine that has drawn many spiritual tourists to Peru. One of my encounters with the huachuma took me far beyond my earthbound identity, revealing a much larger view of the world and the cosmos. The next year, in the course of a single ceremony with ayahuasca in Costa Rica, I experienced such a deep connection with myself and the cosmos that I felt completely at home in my body and on the planet for the first time in my life. Grateful for these gifts, I felt that I was done with the plants and shamans even as I continued to integrate what I had experienced.

The soul and the plants had another agenda. In 2011, I felt called to engage the ayahuasca again. During two trips with Darlene to the Peruvian jungle near Iquitos, I discovered a field of intelligence that lies beyond the visions and physical healing effects for which ayahuasca is known. It was in the first ceremony of 2011 that I heard a voice speak directly and clearly to me. As I described in detail in *The Soul's Critical Path,* the voice clearly instructed me how to relate to the plant in order to access the intelligence that lies beyond the rigorous plant experience itself.

I began to sense that this intelligence uses the plant in a complex variety of ways, one of which is to push aside the brain filters that prevent humans from being overwhelmed by the infinity of gross and subtle informational fields in which we constantly swim. With those filters down—while the analytical brain was intoxicated by the plant, or *moreado,* as they say in this tradition—my soul was able to come forward and hear that field of intelligence speak. The attention skills cultivated over my many years of meditation helped me listen without being overwhelmed by the breathtaking and rigorous healing process that is accompanied by so many physical, auditory and visual effects. What I heard inspired much of *The Soul's Critical Path,* and planted the seed for this book as well.

I returned to the jungle in 2012, hoping to deepen my conversation with this field of intelligence. With more experience behind me, I found myself listening in another way. Without having planned it, I was becoming a critical observer of the phenomenon of which I am now a part: an international spiritual immigration to the jungles and mountains of Peru to taste the medicine and be with the practitioners of various traditions, including *vegetalistas, ayahuasqueros, curanderos, huachumeros,* and pacos—many of whom have adopted for themselves the name *shaman,* a term exported from Siberia and applied to indigenous practitioners throughout the world by anthropologists and spiritual tourists.

I now understood what had called those spiritual tourists to experience the shamans, plants, and pacos. I had been drawn for the same reasons. People had made this spiritual pilgrimage because they wanted to feel better, to heal, and to change their lives. They were responding to a soul-level urge to express, open, connect, grow, sense, taste, transcend, transmute, ascend, descend, awaken, heal, ground, love, trip out, or just be. All of these are urges that reflect the effort of the soul to pull itself together and gain the traction on body and earth that propels the soul on the path of its destiny.

Many of the people who came knew, whether they could articulate their sense of it or not, that their own modern cultures had abandoned the collective cultural soul and their personal souls with it. They sensed that there was support for the soul in Peru.

There is a force of consciousness inherent in the land of Peru. In the places that are not devastated by galloping globalization, it can be found as an openness, a sense of invitation, a voice, a feeling, a tingling sensation, an energy, a direct communication, or a sense of refreshment as dramatic as the cold of a clear mountain stream. Particular plants and places sometimes marked by temples radiate these energies more powerfully. The gift of direct and powerful connection with the intelligence that resides in and behind these places and plants of power is available when we are able to focus and direct our attention with a skill that allows for an open-ended exploration of that connection.

We have an inherent connection with these intelligences, but that connection is without value until we develop the skill of attention that allows us to consciously experience the connection and then elevate it into a relationship. These plants and places create powerful doorways through which soul consciousness can travel when ordinary rational consciousness cannot. The force of this connection is not likely to be experienced by tourists whose attention remains distracted by Western culture.

I sense that there are only a relatively few shamans and pacos with the means to engage this force and introduce Westerners into a working relationship with it. Those that do exist are not easy to find. Westerners are stepping forward, trying to acquire the skills to engage this force as well. Clearly, this force is still accessible in the midst of the global development that continues to deny it, and it has the potential to speed the evolution of human consciousness and enable human survival on this blessed planet. This is why Peru has become, as some have said, the new India for modern spiritual seekers.

As I made my way about Peru, that much seemed obvious.

What I questioned was why the experience of these spiritual seekers seemed to fail to reach the potential that Peru offers. As I watched and listened, it seemed that there were as many horror stories coming out of the experiences—both with the plant medicine and the mountain traditions—as there were stories of changed lives and souls sent more shiningly on their way. There were too many stories of financial and sexual exploitation by the would-be shamans and teachers, unresolved personal issues arising in painful ceremonial experiences without benefit of competent support, occasional suicides, and too much, too soon for those too unprepared, who would take home too little for the effort and expense it took for them to get here.

Yet, while I swayed in the hammock of my jungle tambo and reflected on the parade of spiritual tourists, one group began to stand out. Among these journeyers was a particularly interesting demographic—young, independent women traveling alone in a way that women have rarely traveled the world before recent decades.

Although I met many young men traveling on their own, the nature of their stories seemed to have a very different texture, perhaps more troubled, less focused, more egoistic, more prone to tripping, more about addictions, more anxious, more needful of companionship on the trail, and more resistant to the necessary letting go of the analytic mind. I remembered that, in every meditation and shamanic workshop I had attended over many years, eighty to ninety percent of the participants were women whose ages ranged from mid-thirties into their seventies.

While I was curious about the reasons for this seeming gender difference in this spiritual milieu, itself worthy of attention, I became more fascinated with a particular theme that began to emerge from the stories of the women. I had met a couple of women like these in the States, and now I saw a steady stream of them here in Peru.

What I heard from them was not the oft-recited dichotomies of feminism spoken against the patriarchy: career vs. family, or equal rights and equal pay, or my body and your laws, among others. All of these are critically important issues, but issues that arise nevertheless within the particular frame that the universal patriarchy represents.

That frame is defined, at least in part, by a longstanding corporate control and exploitation of the earth's governments, people, and resources. It is also defined by a deeply rutted habit of seeing the world through the perspective of a man's eye, one that is often directly dominated by an analytical thinking process, or rooted in a testosterone-driven body unregulated by some semblance of a higher consciousness, or both.

The lives of these young women bespoke a rejection of this patriarchal frame at the outset, first as they have let go of nationalistic identities and perspectives, and second as they have come to identify with their soul journeys, with the earth, and increasingly with their own bodies. By shifting identities, these young women have shifted the frame of the discussion, no longer *demanding* what they want from the patriarchal monolith as did many courageous women before them.

Now, they are simply *doing* what they want, leaving the confrontational argument behind—evidencing a growing partnership between the feminine and the masculine within these women. This more balanced internal partnership is more powerful than what is perhaps far more common among women now, which is a shift from a weak feminine to a more powerful embrace of the internal masculine, a stance similar to the unbalanced masculine that the patriarchy already represents. These women have not rejected men. But their own soul journeys seem to have taken precedence over finding a man, even if they were looking forward to encountering one who might be able to step up and truly meet them.

That there are women who have the opportunity and initiative to leave in search of their own souls is one of the richest legacies of a feminist movement that is paradoxically getting lost in the United States by virtue of its failure to think outside the box of the patriarchal corporate imperialism. It does not ultimately serve women for the brightest and best of them to serve on the boards of corporations or in the highest levels of government, when the government and corporations are pursuing policies that are the very means by which women and the feminine are being subjugated and destroyed across the planet. It does not serve the feminine or women for these talented and privileged women to emulate and validate the very male behaviors that are destroying the planet. What ultimate social good is done by women empowered in equal measure with men within the frame of a political and economic power structure devoted to destruction and exploitation of our planet and the most vulnerable of humans on it?

Listening to these different stories of women as deeply as I could in the short time I was able to gather their stories, I thought I heard the elements of an idea that had not yet wholly formed. I felt that these women were sensing their way toward something they could feel but not envision. They were searching in the way that soul navigates, holding attention in the heart, moving toward what resonates, moving forward one step at a time, without the benefit of an understanding of where they were going. I could also see that, while most were unsure what they were searching for and while some were tired, they were determined to stay the course.

As I listened, I sensed—and sometimes hoped and projected—that their lives were reaching beyond conventional American feminist thought to the embodiment and enactment of the far deeper power of the emergent cosmic feminine. While that emergence is finding expression in both sexes, it seems to have more traction at this time among women in general, and perhaps more among a certain group of young women. The women whom I met have enjoyed at least some of the benefits of the education and economic largess that the patriarchy has spread like a thin layer of margarine on a slice of white bread, leaving these young-old souls so hungry for real soul food that they are willing, even eager, to leave home, family, and country to find it.

The themes these women embody include the search for personal freedom, community, and a soul-level identity. None of these themes is new in the evolution of human consciousness, but it seems a new development that there are so many young people embracing those themes in a place where there is a particularly rich soul support for taking a next evolutionary step. In rural Peru, there are plant medicines, living spiritual traditions that remain earth-connected, and the barely fettered openness of the earth itself, all powerfully available to support each of us into the next level of our own soul challenges.

My conversations with these women led me to ask how these extraordinary resources could work better for them in Peru, where this quickening emergence of individual soul consciousness has not been so trammeled by corporate globalization. I wondered more why this movement was working to the benefit of some and not for others. I began to see beyond my own fantasy that some clear or enlightened solutions could be found directly in the remains of the indigenous cultures of the jungle and the Andean cordillera. I began to understand that spiritual tourists were not experiencing some original, pure form of indigenous spiritual practice, but practices that were created in significant part in response to this influx of spiritual tourists. Whatever it is now, it isn't what it was. Foreign money and trans-cultural expectations have changed that. The shamanic know-how of indigenous Peru has become transfigured into something new that makes the old even harder to discover. Yet, there remains old that is golden if one can connect with it.

There are Westerners who stay longer and drink ayahuasca scores, sometimes hundreds, of times with apparently sincere intentions but without clear benefit. There are some who drink once or just a few times and have a transformative experience that they are able to integrate. And there are some who come with the idea that these plant medicines are just another drug on which to trip out.

What was once a sacrament that lent its power to a shaman who prepared the medicine himself for the benefit of others after long apprenticeship can now be acquired with a few dollars in a stall or store almost anywhere in Peru. It can be used without the intermediation of a skilled practitioner, without whom the practice has its dangers.

I was recently told by one longtime observer of the shamanic scene near Iquitos that Western-style medicine had largely supplanted the village shamans two generations ago, making it difficult for the shamans to interest their children in learning skills that required such a long apprenticeship. Much earlier, in 2004, I had heard a similar story from Don Umberto, who said that the children of the Q'ero were not learning the traditions. He encouraged us—the "white people," as he described us—to learn their traditions, take them to North America, and mix and match them.

I heard that the young people in so many villages have been pouring into growing towns with developing economies, deeply affecting the viability of the traditional village cultures and their traditional spirituality. With the new interest from spiritual tourists, however, the shaman and the paco have come into demand anew. I heard that the grandchildren of the shamans and pacos are becoming interested in what their parents had neglected, often because of the financial opportunity their traditions have now created among spiritual tourists. In large measure, these traditions have been commodified.

I watched at close range how spiritual seekers from developed countries were flocking to taste the storied magic of traditions already being abandoned by the transitional culture of this developing country. And I watched how this developing culture was reaching into its own roots to repackage something it could sell to that new audience. This new interest in the powerful medicinal plants and practices of the mountain traditions has created a neo-shamanism that often has only a superficial relationship, for better and worse, with the indigenous practices that had begun to fall away decades before. On the other hand, I suspect that many of the traditional and neo-shamans have little idea of the deep soul impulse that brings Westerners to encounter these traditions, but find in the midst of that impulse an opportunity to sell something to them anyway.

The single constant in this rapidly changing scene is the presence and power of places and plants, and the relative openness of the energies of the land in the rural areas where this cultural exchange is taking place. In the midst of all this change, I saw that some people were getting something of great value, and others not. Watching this process reminded me of watching sausage being made, which seldom inspires a desire to put it in your mouth.

I felt that I could discern two distinct and sometimes overlapping motives for the repackaging this neo-shamanism represents. One was a genuine concern for the need to pass on a rich and indispensable knowledge regarding the relationship between humans, the earth, and the cosmos. The other was a genuine desire to make a buck. Sometimes those motives co-existed in one person.

In one way or another, money has become the sponsor of this new relationship between the tourists from the globalizing cultures and the rising expectations of this culture in the process of being globalized. Money has become the medium of exchange for a process that was never, and ultimately cannot be, solely about the money. Nevertheless, money is playing an indispensable if ambiguous role in the moment of this particular evolution of consciousness. And, despite some hucksterism at one extreme and some wide-eyed gullibility on the other, there is a real need to reciprocate for the value of the exchange in some meaningful way, and there is an opportunity for the process to evolve into something more reliably nutritious than sausage.

I observed a deep irony in this emerging ecotone between two very different cultures. Many young people from developed countries were fleeing the patriarchal cultures that feminist movements had confronted but barely budged. Now these people were seeking guidance and wisdom in a developing country and a spiritual tradition still dominated by a patriarchy far less masked than the one they fled.

I watched as some young women, and more experienced spiritual explorers of both sexes, began to shun the native male shamans who could not control their sexual impulses. There has been an increasing request for or insistence upon working with female shamans or shamans working as married couples, or with the gringos and gringas now increasingly dispensing the medicine. Ironically, but not surprisingly, it has become apparent that some of the male gringo shamans often bring the same unconscious sexual energy to their work, and these may become shunned as well.

The larger irony is that the cultivation of an emergent feminine continues to remain primarily with male teachers. In rejecting this central aspect of the traditional power structure, these young women were mounting a fundamental challenge to the culture to which they had been drawn. I could see in this an emerging dialogue between cultures, but one reflected more by body language than an articulate exchange of ideas. Forces of demand and supply are at work, even if they don't define the real spiritual economy of Peru.

I also saw a mismatch between the short time most of the spiritual tourists had available for an encounter with powerful medicines, and the more prolonged time a significant spiritual transformation requires. The spiritual tourists I met often came for the two weeks their allotted vacations and budgets allowed. Sometimes they come for a bit longer, but still with the expectation they can get what they need in a month or so. In response, the vendors of the spiritual experience have tried to cram numerous plant or other ceremonies into too short a time frame.

There seems an absence of either awareness or concern among many vendors of the medicine of the value of a process of preparation for the encounter, the need to have a skillfully supportive presence during the encounter, and the importance of a process for integrating the encounter. My sense has been that these vendors are often indifferent to the ultimate inadequacy of so few encounters with ceremony when a means of integrating the experiences is absent. Even if these necessities were addressed to the spiritual tourist upon arrival at the place of ceremony, the short time frames are insufficient for the teaching and practice that would support preparation for, presence to, and integration of the experiences that are to come.

Where the spiritual tourism is most dense, there is also a tendency on the part of vendors to cram as many people into a single plant ceremony as the room will hold. Ceremonial spaces are now being built for over one hundred participants. Traditional shamans did not dispense or use the plant medicine this way, and neither contemporary nor traditional shamans are prepared to handle this many clients in a way that connects the client with the potential benefit of the medicine, or to protect the client from the harm that can occur in an unregulated ceremony.

Money, of course, is a primary motivation in such circumstances. Some clients may benefit, but it is a more dangerous practice, for example, than the publication of formerly secret mantras, as occurred in the migration of the Eastern meditation culture to the Western world. In this latter instance, money was sometimes a motivation for spreading the tradition to those whom the traditional teachers would not have earlier accepted, but the concern for spreading consciousness was also a factor. The same mixed motives are present in this Peruvian context.

Even in smaller ceremonial settings, I observed native shamans failing to address issues that arose in ceremony because the issue was beyond the competency of the shaman. Because the plant medicines open the doors of consciousness wide, ceremonies require skilled facilitators who have an understanding of the psychologized modern psyche and who possess the ability to protect participants from the predatory energies that may attend ceremonial settings.

In addition, there is often a language barrier between the facilitator and the participants. That barrier can and does prevent communication of essential information by the shaman, as well as the discovery that the shaman may not have enough understanding of the process the shaman purports to manage. In the morning-after feedback sessions that often follow ceremonies, I have heard the shaman respond to questions with an answer that is accurate but inadequate: "This is a process."

But what *is* the process? How much time does it typically take? What needs to be learned by a Westerner who will be leaving in a few days? The all-too-soon return to a home thousands of miles away often prevents any significant follow-up that might have been helpful or crucial. For many who return home, the time in ceremony seems like a dream. Did it really happen? Did anything happen? And what does it mean for the life I left and to which I have now returned?

Back in the United States, I observed another development. After my first experience with the medicine in 2000, I sought out a teacher of shamanism who could help me understand what I had experienced. I found a teacher in California. My first class of a program that was to eventually last two and a half years had about 100 attendees. I was surprised at this interest in shamanism. What I didn't understand at that time was that I was a participant in a new cultural and spiritual phenomenon in which the passing on of shamanic tradition was now opened to an entirely new audience that had not existed before.

In the villages where shamans have traditionally practiced their professions, shamans represented a singular profession with few ways to enter this work that required the ability to maintain connection with other dimensions for the purpose of protecting the village and healing the villagers. Indigenous shamans didn't teach groups how to journey or how to heal others, even if plant medicines were dispensed to groups for their own healing. Shamans were selected based upon some inherent gift, or a relationship with an experienced shaman or, in the case of the Q'ero tradition, by being struck by lightning. The teaching of the shaman's skills involved a long and arduous apprenticeship.

Now, in North America and Europe, a monumental shift in this teaching tradition had already occurred by the time I registered for class with my credit card. I was naïvely participating in a movement born within the last forty years. Much of what we now see in the teaching of shamanism to Westerners probably started with anthropologist Michael Harner's creation of a teaching program that attempted to distill and transmit practices that are "core," or common to all shamanic traditions. Harner, to his credit, emphasizes that he is teaching technique, not shamans. Nevertheless, the distinction is a fine one that most teachers of shamanism do not make.

I respect Harner's teachings. Yet the movement he has helped to spawn now has spiritual seekers attending workshops in the United States and Europe, with or without a visit to a shaman in Central or South America, that sell the idea that "you too can become a shaman." All you need are a few weekends or some vacation time spread over a year or two, along with sums up to $10,000 or more. I have spent that and more in this pursuit. I have certificates that attest to my attendance. But shamans were never taught or selected in this way. What this new process creates has not been studied, but it is not what existed before. And it is not yet what it can become.

A Peruvian shaman who observed my working with a client on the massage table after observing me in ceremony asked if I was a shaman. It was a good question. I took a moment before responding, finally telling him that I was not. Yet I was something I had not been before I began this investigation more than a dozen years earlier. I knew he had skills I didn't have. I also knew I had skills he didn't have. And we were both working the same street.

We have overlaid the complexity of a modern technological culture onto a waning indigenous culture, and we do not have a measuring stick that might more clearly define the necessary skill set or setting of the shaman who would reach beyond the traditional practice and audience. What a shaman is now, in the emerging global village, is a question and phenomenon that has been the subject of little, if any, study.

Finally, I observed that there is value in all of this, even if the ultimate value and the more elegant, efficient process have yet to emerge. Even as Western culture is rapidly destroying the voice and power of indigenous cultures, the soul that materialistic Western culture denies knows that it has to honor the wisdom of these earlier cultures. Western culture is now challenged to find some new form outside of and beyond those earlier cultures that have become the shell through which something new is now breaking.

In the midst of these observations, one theme began to stand out in my mind. The form this emerging shamanism will take will be deeply influenced by the Westerners who are coming now. Just as Don Umberto had urged in 2004, Westerners are driving the evolution of this spiritual encounter with shamans, pacos, plants, and the deep force of intelligence that lies behind them. They will do so all the more when more of them acquire the skills to touch that force more directly and frequently. I heard this theme affirmed in a prophecy of a jungle shaman related to me by a North American who has been working in this milieu for more than 25 years. More than two decades ago, he said, his own jungle shaman told him that gringos would soon be leading the evolving relationship with ayahuasca.

As I rested and reflected in my jungle tambo, I felt the pressure of that deep force of intelligence pushing for something new and more powerful to emerge. I knew that I was part of a movement that would help to support that emergence. I knew now why people came. This deep force of consciousness called to their souls. The plants called to their souls. Those who listened showed up.

My head started to juggle some separate thoughts.

Souls: Fields of intelligence making an appearance in time, awakening to themselves within a human frame, traveling quickly about the earth with information central to the progress of the evolution of consciousness and creation itself, looking for communities that can support their work. Fast, young messengers looking for places to rest.

Chaskis: Fast, young messengers.

Tambos: Places of rest for chaskis. Planned communities built around a system of communication.

Tribes: The more intentional communities we hope to find when we've left behind the unintentional community that we were born into. What is needed even by very independent souls.

Chakarunas: Old souls who are bridges between this and the other dimensions.

Home: A place to learn and rest. A place we can return to from time to time.

And I thought about invasions.

Dr. Ruben Orellano—a respected Peruvian archeologist, teacher and plant shaman—likes to remind his tourist audiences that are so fascinated with Incan culture that the Incas were only one brief phase of an evolving Andean culture that extends back in time for more than 30,000 years. The Incan culture invaded a pre-existing culture and put its own gloss on it. I see even in Dr. Orellano's life a reminder of a continuing process of invasion. His ancestors came with the Spanish invasion that ended the Incan reign almost 500 years ago and attempted to destroy its shamanic traditions.

More than a century ago, a next invasion by modern globalizing mega-corporations began. That invasion has been accelerated in steroidal fashion in just the last two decades by the introduction of television and the cultural messages that television has pushed so abruptly into the more traditional culture of Peru. Peru is naïve to the dangers of television that research has identified and American culture has also largely ignored.

Marshall McLuhan remains a prophet in this respect, as we can see that the technology is not merely the tool of the new invaders who would use technology to deliver a message, but the substance of the invasion itself. Peru has already been transformed by technology and its direct and addictive impact upon the neurology of its users.

Overlapping with the period of the technological invasion, spiritual tourism is just one more form of what can now be seen as a continually morphing invasion. The souls who have migrated here for their own transformation are also transforming Andean culture by their very presence, by the purpose for which they come, and by the lifestyles and technologies they have introduced to this culture. The whole body of tourism is an invasion. And in less than the blink of an eye, the growing presence of the women with whom I spoke represents another invasion that is affecting the evolution of this Andean tradition.

As I let myself play with these old word-containers and the idea of invasions amidst my fascination with the evolution of consciousness, I found richness in the stories of the women whom I encountered. The stories of these women that I share in the next chapter hint at the potential direction of this continuing evolution, and the communities that will support it.

2

SIX STORIES

Zera

I MET ZERA IN 2005 during a Sandra Ingerman workshop in Santa Fe, New Mexico. Zera was twenty-two years old, probably by ten years the youngest present at this training on soul retrievals. After she and I partnered on one of the exercises, I asked her what had brought her to this particular workshop. She told me she was interested in shamanism and had saved her money for a time to pay the fee.

Zera was relatively itinerant and worked at odd jobs. Her next would be in California, where she could make some quick money cleaning stems in a marijuana processing center. "After that, who knows?" she said. Zera had a boyfriend, but they had separate plans for traveling, and being with him was not her first priority.

I was having a hard time getting my conventional mind around what felt to me like a lack of direction in this intelligent, well-groomed young woman. I asked how she would be traveling to California. She said that she would hitchhike. I felt my daddy alarm go off. "Isn't that dangerous?" I asked. She replied that she had been doing it a long time.

I gathered that Zera had no interest in entering the conventional workforce or getting any further formal education. She managed to do what she wanted to do, and what she wanted was not circumscribed by some long-range plan or goal, but about what interested her at the moment.

"Doesn't this get lonely?" I asked. "Yes," she said. But she was unwilling to give up the sense of freedom that was of foremost importance to her. She also told me that she got tired. But there were things she wanted to learn—about the earth, farming, and living differently from what she saw in her parents' generation.

I asked her, what if there were places with like-minded people where she could trade some labor for some training in the areas of her interest, along with a place she could leave but return to from time to time for rest and connection? She said it would be great to have some rest from her travel, and yes, it would be great to have a way to learn what she wanted to learn with people of her own nature. Then she said that I was the first "older" person to understand what she was feeling.

I don't think I really understood, but I marveled at the courage of this young woman for whom the American Dream held no allure. I was in the process of trying to close down my law practice, but running into a thicket of fears about doing that despite having more money in the bank than Zera could imagine. Could I stop and do what she was doing—on my own, with no backup? No. The American Dream, and the fear that drives it, still held me in its trance.

Grace

I met Grace about the same time. Grace was in her late twenties and had come to me for some help in dealing with the stress of an injury she had sustained when she was knocked off her bicycle by a van. In those days, I had fused shamanic tools, heart-centered meditation, biofeedback, and cranial/sacral techniques in an effort to find a process that resonated with me and provided healing effects for my clients.

Grace wanted to be "normal" in some sense that she projected upon others of her age. She wanted very much to fit in, to find a job that would take her off the financial edge she was living on, and find a relationship with a man who could appreciate her complex nature. Grace felt both physically and emotionally vulnerable.

My own perception was that Grace didn't fit with many of the peers of whom she spoke in the early part of our acquaintance. I saw her as deeply intelligent, with a strong intuitive sense. She had a strong sense of connection with land evidenced in part by her attraction to organic farming. She had an underlying spiritual drive that related, in my opinion, to the vulnerability she felt in the face of the patriarchal culture, and to her inability to fit in with more conventional peers. Not fitting in was a healthy response, I thought, one that derived from the persistent efforts of her soul to emerge.

Our conversations touched upon my own experiences with the shamanic cultures of Peru. I suggested a Peruvian curandero who might be able to help her. Before long, she had saved enough money from her nanny job to get the ticket to Peru, where her interest in organic farming blossomed. She worked with more than one shaman, explored the plant medicines, and made her way on her own. I was in awe of her courage.

I saw in Grace something of the same drive that I had seen in Zera. In Grace, however, there was more ambiguity, at least early in our conversations, about her relationship with the American Dream and its conventions. But I watched as it fell away in direct proportion to her growing sense of self.

Grace spoke to me of her identification with the "queer" movement. She had to explain queer to me, since it is an older derogatory term for homosexual. Queer, she said, has little or nothing to do with sexual orientation. Although the movement had its beginnings in the LGBT community and is in some ways related, Grace explained that queer is not a synonym for gays, lesbians, bisexuals, or transsexuals. Instead, it is a label for an emergent community who see themselves as completely outside the mainstream and who support justice for the entire spectrum of humanity, particularly the disenfranchised. Sexual identity does not equate with political position, she pointed out. Queer is a growing collection of people who *choose* not to fit into the conventional expectations of American culture, and they express that choice at times by "raging against the machine."

As Grace described the queer community to me, it did not seem queer at all. Within this community are people who want to create an environment that will enable them to live in a sustainable relationship with the earth and each other. Those with whom Grace most strongly identified within the queer community were attempting in various ways to recapture indigenous traditions they felt might support them and their own spiritual maturation. These young people wanted the most simple of things: a community in which all were accepted, all paths were honored, and all pulled together in a way of living sustainably with the earth to which our culture remains substantially blinded.

When I asked Grace about her vision of community, she said that she didn't know exactly what it might look like. She had been discussing the same question with her friends. She did say that there were a lot of young people like her, even though she thought they did not form a majority in her generation. Somewhere in those conversations, the notion of "tribe" arose, but I couldn't really relate to it, other than to feel that it would be nice to have a tribe of my own.

In Grace, I found the same courage I saw in Zera, but I was still left with an unanswered question I was as yet unable to articulate. I could only sense that something was up among these young people, and that feeling stuck in my memory.

Sarah

Fast forward a few years.

Darlene and I were a few miles downriver from Iquitos, Peru, sitting on the wooden floor of a jungle *maloka*, the ceremonial space in which the shaman presides over the plant ceremony. Several of us were waiting for a husband and wife team of ayahuasqueros to begin the ceremony of that evening. We had met the wife in ceremony a year earlier near Iquitos.

As we waited, we listened to a story told by Sarah, a woman in her early thirties. We sat in rapt attention as she told of hitching rides to Iquitos from Belgium. She had left her home in search of a South American ayahuasquero, but she was determined not to follow the Internet hype about Iquitos, which she regarded as the business capital of ayahuasca tourism. Instead, she was determined to follow her intuition and be guided to the right teacher in the right place. Then she laughed at herself, recognizing the irony of having traveled so far on intuition to wind up in the same place as those who had come in response to information available on the Internet.

Sarah described herself as a "maybe" professional activist. Her work involved traveling the globe to protest the failure of developed nations and multinational corporations to address or even acknowledge climate change and other environmental disasters for which they bore central responsibility. She described a level of commitment that astonished me.

We listened to her speak about breaking into the final meeting held during a recent global conference on climate change. Doing so required forged credentials and the willingness to push through crowds and security. She described standing on a balcony above where the power players were talking and unfurling a protest banner while she screamed her message.

I did not doubt her story and marveled at her courage. And I felt deeply with her as she dropped her head in the candlelight of our small room, shadow covering her face, wondering out loud whether her work was doing any good. I wondered the same, and yet could not doubt the importance of that work. Without regard for any particular outcome, her passion was inspiring and beautiful to witness.

In the midst of this work, she had taken four months to arrive in Peru. To cross the ocean, she hitched on four sailing vessels—the last of which was crewed by three men. Again, I was overwhelmed by her courage. Sarah was living from her heart, doing what she felt compelled to do. It was heart guidance that had brought her to this small, dark room in a mosquito-infested, wet jungle to discover a deeper way of listening to herself and the guidance of the universe that the ayahuasca experience promises.

I knew what had brought Sarah to this place, because I had heard the same call. And as I listened to her share her story, it was evident Sarah wanted to connect with a community of people who could appreciate the nature of the impulse that had brought her to this experience.

Sarah's story fueled my curiosity, and I realized I wanted to listen to others whom I was meeting on the way.

Heather

A few days later, Darlene and I traveled to another place near Iquitos to work with a different ayahuasquero. There, we met Heather, a woman in her mid-twenties from Australia.

Shortly after completing a degree in acupuncture that included training in China, Heather felt drawn to Peru to experience the ayahuasca. She related that her first encounter with the plant was so profound—in what was expressly a soul-level experience for her—that she decided to move into the world in a more open-ended way. She wanted to see what life "would throw" at her.

Within the space of three years, she managed to visit more than twenty countries in Asia, Europe, and South America. What she encountered affirmed her belief that, by "letting go," life would provide the exact experiences that her soul needed in order to evolve. Looking forward to 2012, her quest was to find her "tribe." Tribes, she said, are global networks that break away from social molds. These networks would help to save her, others like her, and Mother Earth herself. She saw human survival at risk and hoped that the tribes she imagines can use technology and international networking to create small groups of loving potential.

From Heather, I learned that there were, not surprisingly, emerging forms of support for young people doing what she was doing. She spoke of the Internet sites that connected travelers with people willing to loan out a couch, that provided information on where someone could sleep in an airport for free, and that offered assistance in connecting with places where a traveler could perform service in exchange for a place to stay along with some kind of learning experience. Heather had found the center where I met her in just that way. When we met her there, she was serving tables and cleaning up in exchange for the opportunity to drink ayahuasca.

Heather was looking forward to meeting with her boyfriend in a month or two, but she made it clear that her priority was to put herself out into the world, rely on her own resources, and find what was drawing her. Heather said softly that she was learning not to throw herself so hard at the world, not to take a challenge simply because it presented itself, and to be more discerning. As we spoke with her, she was looking forward to her second encounter with ayahuasca.

It was clear from my time with Heather that she was not a tripper—someone who was willing to use whatever drug might take her out of body, into numbness, or into sensation. For Heather, this impending encounter with the ayahuasca was a matter of compelling curiosity. She wanted to find out more about herself and had come in the faith that the plant would provide her that access.

I asked about her notion of tribe. Heather replied that she was quite past the point of getting together to exchange stories or small talk. She wanted to walk with people who were consciously choosing a path of exploration. "Soul" was clearly a word with which she resonated. She saw herself as a soul.

In my conversation with Heather, the words "soul" and "tribe" came together. A new idea was rippling the surface of my mind.

Jane

When Darlene and I returned to Peru's Sacred Valley a few weeks later, we met Jane in Pisac, a small village that experiences daily busloads of tourists who come to the village plaza to buy old and new. Pisac has an international cachet. It has become a hub for the large numbers of young people who come to Peru to experience the plant medicine. Ayahuasca and huachuma have also migrated here from their places of origin. In Pisac, the extent of plant-medicine tourism has caused many locals, including transplanted young people, to become cynical about the use of these plants.

Jane was friendly and open, initiating conversation with us across a large communal table at Ulrike's Restaurant, a landmark for the travelers who pause in the Sacred Valley. Jane told us she had just arrived in Pisac after a stay at a high-altitude ayahuasca retreat in central Peru.

In that center, Jane said, the vision was to combine Buddhist meditation perspectives with an intensive daily encounter with ayahuasca and other plant *dietas*. A dieta involves drinking a tea made from a plant for a period of several days or weeks. The purpose is to explore whether the plant and the body share an affinity for each other that might strengthen the body, and to see if the plant might ally with the ayahuasca to enhance the healing effect of the ayahuasca upon the body itself.

Jane was stimulated by her experience there, but had left in response to what she described as an overabundance of masculine energy. She was the only woman in a core group otherwise made up of men, among whom she experienced a certain rigidity and absence of personal insight despite their innovative and disciplined approach to the medicine.

Jane was thirty-five and had left her home in Ireland fourteen years earlier to start a career in investment banking in London. She said she found herself "caught up" in a lifestyle in which making money and living the high life were her priorities. Within a few years, she was diagnosed with tuberculosis. In the face of that challenge, she began making what she characterized as "small" changes in her life, although I found them not small at all.

She began practicing yoga and meditation, attending spiritual workshops, and reading books of a spiritual nature. She was excited to meet people who taught her a different perspective about life. Among these new experiences, she singled out her encounter with Reiki as a turning point, saying it gave her a sense of subtle energy that she had not previously experienced. As I heard this, I reflected upon how many people had told me that Reiki was an introduction to subtle energies and a spiritual unfoldment that might follow.

Jane treated the tuberculosis with antibiotics, and she took an extended trip to Thailand to rest and recover. She expressed some feeling of guilt about the use of conventional medicines at a time when she was opening to alternative approaches to supporting her health. In Thailand, she decided to return to London and her job in order to save the money that would enable her to leave.

And leave she did. After a total of seven years of work in banking, Jane started an odyssey that returned her to Thailand. There, she rock climbed, fell in love, and moved on with her mate to Alaska, where she worked as a carpenter and crewed on a fishing boat. She thrived on the hard labor. After two years, she returned with her mate to Thailand, where she began to experience some suffocation of her desire to travel to new places as he vacillated.

She left the relationship, completed a Vipassana intensive, and continued the Vipassana silence while travelling through Thailand, Laos, and Cambodia for two months. With that time of reflection behind her, she decided to try again with her mate, who traveled for three months with her to India. The relationship faltered once more against the tide of her desire to continue her exploration of the world. She returned to Ireland for a visit with her family while she worked out her next move.

The next move took her back to India, where she trained in yoga and Ayurvedic medicine for several months. Then she traveled to Nepal, staying for two months and traveling part time with a female friend. In Nepal, she trekked the Annapurna circuit alone for seventeen days.

From Nepal she flew to Guatemala, where she started her search for a shaman from whom she could learn about natural healing. At Lake Atitlan, she became frustrated, discovering that most of the shamans were heavy drinkers. Hearing her experience, I remembered I had heard there is a high incidence of alcoholism among traditional shamans around Iquitos.

Jane moved on to Belize, then to Nicaragua, where she worked as a massage therapist for several months. From Nicaragua she traveled to Costa Rica, again staying for an extended time and working as a massage therapist and yoga teacher until feeling the call to return to Alaska.

In Alaska, Jane married, staying for two years before she was overcome by the feeling that she was not living her life's purpose. After some discussion, Jane and her husband hauled their belongings down the coast and through the northwestern United States, punctuating the trip at the Burning Man Festival. From there, they returned to her home in Ireland, then on to Scotland. Her husband had gone to school in Scotland and became excited about continuing his education there. Jane, however, again felt that the relationship was hindering her dream, and they parted. She returned alone to South America and on to Peru. After five months of travel, she found herself in Pisac.

Jane's dream is to live and work in a healing center that uses plant medicines. She feels strongly that there is a need to bridge these powerful medicines with Western ways of healing. She wants to learn to make teas, tinctures, and other herbal remedies in order to complement the healing methods that she has already learned in the course of her travels.

Listening to Jane's story, I again found myself quite blown away. How rare it was a mere few decades ago for a woman to travel in this way, and now I was encountering several who had crossed my path in a relatively short time.

Jane's story of the effort to combine Asian meditation techniques with the ayahuasca experience resonated with my own experience and the message of *The Soul's Critical Path*, which emphasized the need for a skill of attention sufficient to receive the gifts that the plant medicines are ready to offer.

Soul tribes and tambos? Interesting idea, she said.

Robin

Another month or so down the road, I met Robin and her male partner Darcy at a huachuma ceremony that took place near Pisac. They were five years into their relationship and talking of marriage.

Robin was thirty years old. She had been traveling the world on her own since she was fifteen, when she left her home in the U.S. to study in Australia. At seventeen, she went to Mongolia with a nonprofit that worked with orphans and street people. By age nineteen, she was living in Nepal and traveling throughout Asia on her own. During this entire time, she was experiencing serious endocrine challenges that her many U.S. doctors had been unable to diagnose. Robin told me that she was determined not to let her health deter her from her desire to experience the world.

What drove her, and continues to drive her, she said, is "a deep knowing that, for the whole of my life, I existed before this body/mind, that I came here for a reason, and that I am dedicated to fulfilling this to the best of my ability as the human I find myself."

She remembers the day she was born, a memory she says has guided her life in a number of ways. "Right after my birth," she said, "I remember looking up and seeing the silhouetted figures of a number of people. What rose up through me was curiousness about where I was and who or what those beings were. As a little child I would constantly remember this experience. I came early to the conclusion that, to wonder where I was, I must have come from somewhere else. It felt that there was much more to life than just being human."

Robin began to question the nature of existence at age four. Reflecting on her many memories of her early life, she recalls looking in the mirror and saying to herself, "This is not me, I am not this person. But who am I?" She said that this deep curiosity has been an innate part of her being for all of this life. "I want to see," she said, "what is around the next turn." She said that "a sense that life is very precious" pervades her life.

At twenty-two, she found herself alone in Siberia, suffering from an especially acute attack of a longstanding uterine condition that she now says had its roots in environmental pollution. That diagnosis evaded conventional medicine and more than a dozen doctors. Alone, she made her way across Russia and Europe to get home again.

Talking to Robin now, I saw an incredibly intelligent, articulate, and driven woman. Listening to her story, it was apparent that, by facing the pain of her physical condition, she turned it into a force that drove her to take responsibility for understanding the problem on her own. She became a voracious researcher, educating herself in alternative remedies. And she became an avid follower of the work of Byron Katie, whose rigorous process of self-inquiry provided a framework in which Robin subjected her own mental processes to the same degree of examination to which she was subjecting her body.

Robin's story unfolded for me in the midst of a huachuma ceremony. This powerful plant medicine can have many effects. I had taken a small dose on that day. The medicine had brought me to a place in my own heart from which I could be present, feel connection with her and my surroundings, and listen. Robin and I sat in the ceremonial maloka for hours as I gently inquired, and she openly shared. There was something much more powerful underlying Robin's drive than the pain that so consumed her attention. While pain forced her attention to her body and her mind, what she found in this unlayering of body and mind was another, deeper level of searching, one that rose to meet her. My own work and experience has brought me to the knowing of what arises from beneath, and it is what I have called the soul, as others have.

The soul impulse in Robin brought her to Peru and the plant medicine. She has told her own story in excruciating terms on her

Internet site. She relates how the plant medicine took her attention more deeply yet, clearing her of the toxins and their effects on her body. She tells a story of how her growing relationship with the plant created a new context in which her process of mental inquiry could integrate this healing into a new perspective of the world and the cosmos. For me, her story represented a singularity. She had come to what I have called a *soul perspective*—what I had described in *The Soul's Critical Path* as the necessary condition of the soul's emergence from its fate into the path of its destiny. If our work is to mature, our sense of who we are has to shift from its historical identification with the personality to the soul itself.

Reading her blog written several years ago about her experience in ceremony with huachuma, I found some jewels that she consented to my sharing here.

> *I knew absolutely in these moments (and this clarity has not waned since) that my role here is to birth this consciousness onto the planet again. To dedicate my time-energy-consciousness to co-creating more spaces on the planet that house this vibration of awakened mind.*
>
> ...
>
> *I was shown the birth of four worlds, each birthed from the previous and while traits remained constant, the worlds were radically different. Each world was an evolution of the previous; each species carried traits of its old skin, but was radically different. I saw how these worlds emerged out of each and every point in the multi-verse, each moment a welling up and spreading out of time-space-consciousness. The emerging of a new world was the Creatrix evolving. It was the whole changing, metamorphosing. Change the ever-constant truth. I was brought to the present and into the near future where another age is to be birthed. What that will look like I was not privy to, but I saw*

great change on a physical scale. The planet rapidly reorganizing itself, with humans not being the center of this change, integral because we are consciousness, but not central. I was shown a community where people came from around the world to learn to align themselves to change, to learn to "sing the world into being." Darcy and I stood at the base of a huge huachuma in full bloom welcoming family, friends, and strangers. This I was informed was both metaphorical and literal. I was told that I am supposed to work with him to create a community dedicated to this. That this is just one of the many things we will do together as life partners. I found out later that he was informed of exactly the same thing. We had at this point only been traveling together for two weeks, with no conversation ever being had about love or commitment. And yet neither of us doubted it for a moment or has since.

I saw that there will be many such centers, and that in this world evolution there will be many types of experiences all okay and integral to the larger process. Some will find it hard to adapt to a rapidly changing environment or choose not to adapt. While others will ride the wave change, embracing the endless possibilities presented. It was made very clear to me that each has the right to choose, and each of us does choose each moment how we focus our attention and intention. To ride the wave, I must focus on the razor edge of duality, choosing my experience in this endless dark and endless light, holding each, while consciously watching the now flow through me. My body began to calm, and I came back to the small hostel room, the flat bed, and my breath. Nothing, absolutely nothing after this day would be the same. I had been given the gift and responsibility of vision.

The time I spent at Chavin [comment by JPD: Chavin is a temple in the central highlands of Peru that *is more than 3000 years old, also known as Chaupin, and regarded as a birthplace of the use of huachuma] has altered my perception of reality, and how I perceive my role as a co-participator in this consensual world reality. I have learned that when one willingly embraces the fires of transformation, the fear of death, and relinquishes all hope of external salvation for the love of truth, the universe responds in kind with gifts of understanding and a path of purpose. After this point I realized that the time for growth is now, and began to dedicate each day to learning and sharing as much as possible about healing consciousness.*

. . .

This path is about embracing the potentiality of being human, and in order to do this all areas of my life must be focused on cultivating a soil of self in which this blossoming can occur unhampered. Everything from nutrition, to what information I am taking in, to the quality of my relationships, to where I focus my attention. This is a path of unification and healing. Huachuma made it clear what activities I had been participating in that were no longer appropriate. It is the time to be clear and centered; it is the time to embrace more of the potentiality that this life offers. What always surprises me is that when it is truly time to let a thing go, when an activity or relationship has run its course, releasing it is effortless and a joy. Nothing forced, all things serve us, until they don't, and then new things do. Wonderfully and idiotically simple, but so true. Some things must die for others to be born.

I had written much of this book when I met Robin. I had already conceived of the notion of soul tribes and the communities that I have given the name tambos. And now I saw that my soul had touched the same fields of other-dimensional consciousness that Robin had visited. I knew that I had captured an idea, and that it had captured me as it had captured Robin.

3
MANY TRIBES

ALL OF US live in a tribe.

We may not feel like we fit in the tribe we have, but we all have one. We might think that comfort is a sign of tribal membership, but discomfort is just as much a sign. Not fitting in is as much an indication of a tribal relationship as is fitting in, and not fitting in is a gift just the same. Just as tribes reflect who we are, they also reflect who we are not. Tribes provide the mirror we need to stimulate the emergence of our souls.

We all have more than one tribe. Wherever we live, we tend to seek the tribe that is most reflective of who we are, and we yearn to leave the one that wants us to be something we aren't. When we friend on Facebook, we are tribing. When we go to meetup. com, we are tribing. Whatever we are interested in doing, we tend to tribe-up when we do it. Hikers find hikers. Meditators sit with meditators. Dancers do it with dancers. Thinkers are more comfortable with other thinkers. Runners run with runners, and some of us run with the wolves, at least if the wolves tribe us. We always know it when we get tribed and when we get un-tribed.

A tribe is a relationship—a twosome plus. A friendship creates tribeship. A family is a tribe. You and your dog and cat form a tribe. Bowling leagues and political parties are tribes. Neighbors and football fans form tribes. Towns and cities are tribes. Nations are tribes. Humans are one big tribe made up of sub-tribes.

The smallest human tribe on the planet—and the most fundamental—is the one formed between your soul and your body. Souls have an infinite quality, while bodies exist in time and space. Speaking simply of what is an infinitely more complex relationship, souls and bodies find their connection through an interdimensional portal that we sometimes call the heart.

Through that portal, embodied souls also experience their connection to other tribes beyond time/space. There are soul groups that incarnate together. There are soul families to which souls return. And there are other-dimensional beings who await your attention at the threshold of time/space because they have made your soul destiny their concern. These include the heaven fields of intelligence we have called guides and angels, as well as those fields we sometimes recognize as cosmic archetypes that also bless our consciousness from time to time with their direct presence.

These helper beings from other dimensions also include earth fields of intelligence. We know them as the spirits of plants, animals, mountains, winds, water, fire, and earth itself. Ayahuasca and huachuma are portals to fields of intelligence in other dimensions beyond our own. All of these fields of intelligence can tribe us. Each of these fields offers the opportunity for the deep sense of connection we seek when we go tribing.

The Q'ero carry portable altars called *mesas,* made of handwoven fabrics called *mestanas.* Like the practices of shamans of other traditions, these altars contain various ceremonial tools. Among these tools are stones, meteorites, crystals, and other objects that act as transistor-like amplifiers of energetic connection to those other-dimensional fields of intelligence that have tribed these shamans. In my own mesa, I carry similar objects of amplification that represent some of the spirit tribe members with whom I have sought to maintain connection and whose help I call upon. The makeup of my spirit tribe has changed over many years, just as my own tribal connections in the ordinary world of time/space have ebbed, flowed, or passed on.

Within the boundaries of larger tribes, such as cities, we head for the smaller tribes made up of people who are more like us and are more likely to accept, allow, and love us. Sometimes we need those larger tribes to find a critical mass of people sufficient to form the smaller tribe that is more like us. This is why so many young people have fled small towns that couldn't contain the largeness of their souls. When we leave the tribe of our original family, we are often looking for the place where we hope our next tribe will be gathering.

When I left my small birth community as a teenager headed for college in the larger city, I was intent upon finding my tribe, although I didn't understand it in that way then. And when I left the same community again at age 60, I was again intent upon finding my tribe, but quite consciously this latter time. The tribal connections I continue to find now look very different from my earlier tribes, which is often true for souls who continue their work of taking over the job that the personalities formerly performed. As we change and grow, the texture of our tribal connections changes also.

Tribes of every size have two qualities. The first is *culture:* a set of intangibles that are *shared*, such as beliefs, ways of seeing, customs, worldviews, things done together, and experience or history. Do we watch soccer or American football? Do we value work more than play? Is our United States nation/tribe, as a twelve-year-old girl in India asked me, a warring nation or a peaceful nation? What is our relationship to science? What are our beliefs about God? How do you feel about a burger and fries? Do you eat cows or carrots? What do we believe about wealth, economic growth, the importance of the stock market, and the idea of progress?

The second quality of tribes is a *place:* a territory that the tribe calls its own. In the tribe of two or a few, that territory may be what we call home. In the tribe of a nation, that territory is the homeland. Distinct place has historically led to distinct culture, the combination of which lends itself to a nation/tribe seeing itself as unique among other nation/tribes, even as it may tribe other nations with agreements concerning place ("We won't invade yours if you don't invade ours."). North Americans have emphasized their relationship with Britain in the past because of similarities in culture (common beliefs and genetics among the dominant class, for example). And we have made war more easily in the Middle East where the interests in common are not so apparent to our narrow tribal way of thinking. Dropping bombs is a clear way of un-tribing.

The economic prosperity enjoyed by the United States has become a distinguishing feature of America's culture and integral to its beliefs and behaviors. As the American Dream became embedded in our consciousness, people began to spend more and more time working in order to create the prosperity which the dream envisioned, leaving less time for other pursuits. The collective desire to grow prosperity—indeed, the belief in growth itself as possible, necessary, and always for the common good—has caused ever-increasing competition for resources among the nation-tribes. While this may have always been true to some degree among tribes, it is more dangerously true now, since increasing competition for global resources amidst overpopulation now threatens the very viability of humans on the planet.

The focus on prosperity has had another effect. Prosperity has allowed for inter-nation-state travel in a way that has allowed cultural distinctions to diminish. More people are becoming citizens of the world, and their identification with nation states is diminishing. As we move around the world, we learn that people are the same in important ways, which causes a melding of world culture in increasing ways. Communications technology is driving this melding process at an unimaginable pace. We are communicating with each other in a way that has never happened before. But nation-tribes remain. And standing in their shadows are powerful corporate tribes that do not welcome the economic changes the ecology of our planet demands.

For every tribe of every size, there exists a shared understanding, an agreement about *how* we will be together. For every tribe, there is a shared place—some *where* we are together, even if that space is virtual, such as is now developing on the Internet. We are born into that first agreement and place. As I explained in detail in *The Soul's Critical Path,* that first agreement, and the family with whom we will enact it, were set up for us and constitute a central part of our fate.

As the soul awakens to the memory that it *is* a soul, it also begins to discover the nature of its fate. Along the way, the awakening soul will discover the particular agreements that it made with other souls before it entered the body. The soul's ability to discover those agreements reflects the degree to which the soul is able to discover and enact the agreement the soul has made with itself—which is to pursue its own destiny. So, while the tribe into which a soul is born is part of that soul's fate, the soul's impulse is to find the tribe that will support the soul's engagement with its destiny.

On my own path, there have been no tribal connections more powerful than the relationships that I have had with women. These tribes-of-two form connections that are intimate in direct proportion to the depth of the soul skills and soul perspective that we bring to these encounters. These connections, like all other tribal connections, involve an agreement, either express and conscious or unconscious and implicit.

In retrospect, I can see the agreement each relationship represented, and how those agreements were a clear mirror of the degree to which my soul had emerged and matured. The nature of intimacy experienced by a personality that is standing in for a slumbering soul is far different from the nature of intimacy experienced by a mature soul that has stepped forward to manage the personality in conscious partnership with the body.

The intimacy between more mature souls requires more spaciousness, respect, presence, independence, and depth. For immature souls, intimacy evokes the mirror of discord, conflict, reactivity, and the pain that—driving us apart or not—might drive us more deeply into our own self-inquiry and the possibility of greater soul emergence.

As I reflected upon the process of my becoming acquainted with Peru and its culture, both past and present, I watched my own identification with my nation-tribe begin to diminish. The same happened with my relationship with the small coal-mining community in New Mexico where I was born and lived for longer than fifty years. I could see and appreciate my roots and connection to the people of that town.

I remembered playing in the hills and feeling nurtured by the sun-warmed dirt and stone outcrops. I remembered the rites of passage for teenage boys that involved fast driving, binge drinking, and playing football, the latter two rendering me unconscious at times. I remembered my feelings of deep affection for the many people I had been with for so long.

I knew the stories of so many people with such intimacy that I could not, in more recent years, walk down a street without being flooded with decades of memories that were associated with this house or that building or this trail up a hill. There was a momentum in the consciousness of the place, and much of it was like a warm bath for me. For my personality, there was comfort in the known of this place and its people. For my soul, however, there was the deep pain of not belonging there any longer, a pain that finally propelled me along a path illuminated by my heart.

Like Jane, I felt a sense of suffocation in that place that grew more and more intense over time. It was my tribe, and it was not my tribe. This small town had supported me, and I it. It had mirrored me in every way as I returned from increasingly frequent explorations of new horizons, while remaining based there to continue my law practice and raise my family.

When my children moved on, and my marriage of thirty years wound to its close, my soul felt the need to move out even more. A 1998 trek in Nepal yielded an entirely new perspective about how people still survive in small groups on subsistence farming, but I had no mental framework for integrating that information. Years of traveling to Peru began to loosen my relationship with my former tribe by offering the view of another, different kind of tribe that spoke to my soul. My emerging community gradually became more spread out, as I was led to multiple places where I could connect with other people of like mind and heart. A single geographical place did not seem to have an allure for my soul. My soul was finding its place in the geography of my body, and my body was becoming more mobile as my soul began to push the personality around the world.

Rocking in the gentle motion of my hammock in my jungle tambo in 2012, I realized that my tribal affiliations had changed. The soul/body tribe had become primary. The soul was finding its home in the body, and the body was finding its home again on the earth. Now, on an extended trip to Peru, whatever place I found myself in from time to time became my temporary place of tribe and my home of the moment.

My relationship with my adult children had become more distant. I deeply missed them and my young grandchildren, but I knew there was reason for the stretching of those tribal relationships, and those reasons would become more clear as time passed. This evolving experience of tribal connection was itself deeply affecting the form of the new idea that was beginning to fill these old containers of *tribe* and *tambo*.

Something more was emerging.

4

STAGES OF TRIBAL CONSCIOUSNESS

EVERY HUMAN HAS a particular mindset and lives in a particular setting. Our individual mindset is the whole of the beliefs that we hold in our physical body, emotions, and mind, which is a continuum that we often call personality. Our setting is our experiential environment that continues to offer itself as new material for consideration of our mindset. That environment is not only geographical, but cultural (the beliefs held by culture), electromagnetic, and multi-dimensional.

These two elements are interactive: what we experience influences what we believe, and what we believe influences what we experience. In the same way, these two elements—set and setting—provide a basis for understanding that a tribe also holds beliefs in common among its members who also share a common experience of the world. In that way, we can speak of *tribal consciousness.*

My notion of tribal consciousness is analogous to the stages of consciousness that individual souls experience. I have attached an appendix, taken from Chapter Two of *The Soul's Critical Path,* which summarizes soul stages of evolution in more detail. This provides a quick reference for the nature of these distinct stages.

Astrologers can chart the personality and trajectory of a nation-tribe, based upon the time of its birth, just as the personality of an individual is charted. Similar to an individual, a nation-tribe has unconscious elements in its personality. There are unresolved issues and conflicts. It has a history, and it has a story. It may even have a destiny, if it can transcend the fate that challenges individuals and nations alike.

A nation-tribe can respond as a collective, such as happened with America's entry into World War II, or following the tragedy of 9/11. The tribe of a nation can feel anger, despair, elation, and all of the other emotions that individuals feel, because the energy of a nation is the collective of the energies of the individuals that make it up.

If the small tribes that make up the nation-tribe find themselves in agreement, then their combined energy is very powerful, as occurred in those two instances. As the small tribes that make up the nation-tribe splinter, the feelings of the nation-tribe will be conflicted, as happened with the United States' mood regarding the Vietnam War. We can see in the ramp-up to presidential elections that the political parties fan the flames of emotion in order to enlist the power of some tribes, while pitting them against other tribes within the larger nation-tribe.

Like an individual soul, a nation-tribe can operate at various skill levels. It can be more or less conscious, and more or less intentional. It can adapt and change, or fail to do so. It can move forward under the influence of an enlightened vision, or fail to have one. In the United States, many souls are quite awake. These individual souls can see the pathology of the country's trajectory, but there is apparently not a sufficient mass of such souls to shift our present trajectory.

There is an important difference between individual souls and tribes. Souls can *evolve*, but tribes *form* around a particular stage of soul consciousness that reflects an average collective consciousness of the souls making up the tribe. When a critical mass of individual souls evolves to a new level, new tribes may form from those evolving souls who have separated from the old tribe. We saw this at a national level when the American colonies separated from the tribe of Great Britain and did so with a vision of creating a culture based in a dream of greater freedom—a vision that came from a few more highly evolved souls who found an opportunity for the collaboration that became the basis for the new tribe.

Stage One

Tribes that form from souls which have themselves evolved to higher stages of soul consciousness mirror and parallel the several stages of individual soul evolution that I have described in *The Soul's Critical Path*. In that earlier book, I repeated Plato's story of how souls are gathered before they take birth on earth in order to prepare for that journey. At that juncture, what I called Stage One soul consciousness, souls are self-aware. They know that they are souls, even if they have not achieved the wisdom that their future evolution promises. At that stage of individual soul awareness, the soul families that meet and greet between incarnations are also self-aware of their soul status. Some families are groups of more evolved individual souls, and their meetings are more purposeful as they choose their challenges in the incarnation to come. Some of these souls incarnate in groups, and they may choose a nation-tribe into which they will come.

Stage Two

As Plato's story continues, he relates that the fate of individual souls is set by the three Sisters of Fate beneath the whirling spindle that is the symbol for the astrological influence of the position of the planets and stars at the moment of birth. Plato told how, before souls departed for the planet and the bodies that awaited them, they were made to drink from the River of Forgetting. In Plato's telling of the story, some souls drank more, and some drank less. The memory that we are souls is more deeply buried, Plato might have been suggesting, for those of us who drank more. Robin's story suggests that her soul drank less, as one might imagine for each of the other five women whose stories I have shared.

Hidden in this forgetting is a secret. Part of this secret is the karmic setup we call *fate*. Fate is the inevitable group of challenges that a soul has to overcome in order to reveal the other part of the secret, which is the soul's not so inevitable destiny—a destiny that has to be tracked down, grown into, created in collaboration with the universe, and enacted in a skillful collaboration with the body. The majority of souls on the planet remain in the sleepy state of forgetfulness, and the tribes to which they belong reflect this stage of unconsciousness as well. A nation-tribe that is composed predominantly of people who do not remember that they are souls is itself without a soul. In differing degrees, the nation-tribes of the planet are characterized by this level of forgetfulness.

At this time, the United States' rather unconscious personality believes itself to be a world leader offering to share prosperity based in principles of democracy and capitalism. Much of the rest of the world sees the United States caught in an egotistic blindness to its own internal conflicts, hypocritically preaching democracy while submitting to the control of corporations that drive national policies that are imperialistic, environmentally unsustainable, exploitive, and genocidal.

If the United States still has a soul, it is deeply asleep within a body that is managed by a personality that projects upon the rest of the world responsibility for the increasing pain that it is suffering within—the within that is made up of the American people. Our nation-tribe is asleep, caught in its fate, unaware that its potential destiny cannot emerge without the national soul awakening to who it is.

Stage Three

In *The Soul's Critical Path,* I related how individual souls can awaken from Stage Two consciousness into Stage Three consciousness, which culminates with the clear experience of *being* a soul. At this juncture, a soul comes to a full remembrance of the answer to the question, "Who am I?" As Stage Three consciousness arrives, we *know* in our hearts and souls that we are souls, an *experiential knowing quite beyond mere belief* that we are souls.

When the soul has awakened to the memory of who it is, it has arrived at a critical and important juncture, but there is much work yet for the soul to do. Despite reaching what might have appeared from below as a pinnacle, the end of Stage Three turns out upon our arrival to be a plateau from which other heights and depths loom.

The now awake soul still needs to clear out the habits and patterns by which its personality has adapted to the soul's fate, adaptations that reflect the personality's misunderstanding of who it is and why it is here. Those misunderstandings arise from childhood and adult traumas the body has suffered without the benefit of a soul perspective. These traumas have resulted in the creation of patterns of behavior—defensive strategies the immature personality adapted to protect itself from further trauma—that need to be cleared and healed in order to bring the body to the receptive and trusting state of feeling loved and safe.

Without that healing, the body cannot collaborate with the soul. And the soul still needs to acquire the deeper skill of gathering all of its attention to itself, consolidating its identity as a soul, holding itself in the heart field in direct proximity to the body, and learning to inhabit the surface personality for the purpose of bringing the body into full collaboration with the soul's purpose.

Between the forgetfulness of Stage Two and the clear awakening that culminates in Stage Three for individual souls, many small tribal relationships form. We tribe with counselors, healers, personal partners, alternative-medicine practitioners, workshop leaders, yoga instructors, qi gong teachers, meditators, and vegetarians, to name just a few.

The conversations heard within these tribes concern issues of personality: positive versus negative thinking, victim thinking, attitudes about suffering, the dynamic of projection, the need to take responsibility for emotional reactions, and so on. These tribes search the Internet and bookstore flyers for other "spiritual" people. That search has created the huge market for self-help books.

These are all tribes that have begun to step out of the Stage Two tribe. But when an individual soul comes to a full, experiential remembrance of who it is, it becomes difficult to find a tribe that provides a full measure of support for the next steps these souls need to take.

As I observe the spiritual milieu of Peru, I see souls at various levels between Stage Two and the culmination of Stage Three. My sense is that there are many awakening souls here, but relatively fewer even within this group that experience themselves as souls. I saw these strong and purposeful women whose stories I have shared as hovering around the culmination of Stage Three consciousness—almost to the experience that they are souls, just coming into it, or moving just beyond it.

I see them looking for the tribe that consists of equally self-aware souls with whom they can connect, share, explore, find support, and be mirrored. It is not apparent that these tribes have formed beyond a loose network or a particular personal relationship, but it feels like a vision is emerging that would encourage the formation of new tribal communities that they are seeking. This is what Robin has envisioned, even if the specific form of that community was not yet clear.

In the ayahuasca centers, I saw an emergent prototype that begins to address these soul needs. At the same time, looking at these efforts from a soul perspective, I could also see the insufficiency of these initial efforts. The word *ayahuasca* itself refers to the soul as its central concern. Yet I heard precious little discussion of the soul, its nature, its relationship to the body, or how the plant engages the soul process.

More present is the traditional focus on healing, without a clear understanding that the healing is a pre-condition to an emergence of soul destiny, rather than the mere relief of the physical or psychological discomfort that is often the motivation for the personality to bring the body to this rigorous jungle experience. Still missing is a vision large enough to guide the relationship between humans and the plant medicine to its potential with respect to the evolution of consciousness from a soul perspective.

There are other perspectives in play. One perspective reflects traditional shamanic perspectives about healing, which touches both physical and soul levels, but does not reach to an evolutionary soul perspective. There is also the psychological perspective that has followed the spiritual tourists into the jungle, one that looks more consciously at historical traumas and adaptive patterns, in addition to the addictions that traditional shamanism attempts to treat.

There is also an expansive perspective that comes to modern Western spirituality from Asia, which concerns itself with subtle bodies and energy systems. This Asian perspective coincides with traditional shamanic perspectives that see a need to address our issues at the level of subtle energy.

However, it appears to me that the present approach to the soul work in this Peruvian milieu is missing the understanding that the maturation of the soul requires a disciplined skill-development process that requires us to learn how to control attention and where to place it. When we learn to gather attention back to the soul and anchor the soul at the threshold of the portal I have called the heart field, then we can learn to direct the soul's attention anywhere it needs to go for the support and guidance that souls require. Only if we shift attention from healing the personality to healing the soul can we arrive at that level of soul maturity in which the soul can lead the process of healing the personality.

Also missing are more coherent answers to the questions "Who am I?" and "What is my purpose?" that guide us to shift our personal identities from the default personality to that of an emerging soul. Only when we see ourselves as emerging souls that need a working relationship with the body in order to create a destiny of purpose on the planet can we see the value in all of these perspectives. Only then can we begin to see the elements of a larger strategy of soul support that, when combined, speed the evolution of souls by drawing out the greater potential of the plant medicines in the context of a more conscious relationship with the earth and a collaboration with *her* soul.

These necessaries define the mission of soul tribes. The integration of these approaches combined with a skillful collaboration with the plant medicines may offer an efficient and faster-paced engagement with our own souls and the process of the further evolution of consciousness.

Stage Four

It is clear that the communities that would fully support Stage Four souls have not yet manifested. So what is Stage Four for souls? With this experiential soul perspective gained at the culmination of Stage Three, the soul can then enter into Stage Four consciousness, which entails the real work of helping the body discover a sense of feeling safe and loved. A sense of love and safety, consciously experienced by the body, sets the stage for the deeper healing that involves dispatching those patterns that arose around early traumas.

At this juncture, the soul has to develop the skills of attention that are the very means by which the soul can channel the heart-based sense of love and safety the body requires. Developing the skills of attention necessary to create this sense of love and safety in the body requires discipline and benefits from skilled support. The work of dispatching the experience of trauma held unconsciously in the body is also benefitted by skilled support.

The plants offer themselves to play a significant role in all of this, but the infrastructure for combining the potential of the plants with the support for these soul needs is not in place. For Stage Four souls, the supportive tribes may consist of a friendship here or there, a special relationship in which two souls see and honor each other's commitment to their own respective soul's journey, or a relationship with a teacher who has moved beyond Stage Four herself. A State Four tribe needs a program of support that works from a soul perspective.

Stage Five

The plateau of Stage Four consciousness is like the high place we have climbed in order to dive into the sparkling ocean of Stage Five consciousness. Stage Five begins after the soul has developed the skill of controlling its attention, has subsumed the personality, and has helped the body to release the defensive patterns arising from early wounding.

Stage Five represents the deeper dive into a relationship with the body that makes the body fully available to the soul's work of destiny. The soul must develop a collaborative relationship with the body in order to bring the body's power into service of the soul's purpose. When that occurs, there is an explosion of passion—felt in the field of the heart and in the chest of the body—that fuels the soul's forward movement on the trajectory of its destiny. The pursuit of this destiny requires a further and yet deeper dive through the body into the density of matter where the work of creation can be moved forward, informed by heaven and formed from the matter of *mater* earth.

Stage Five soul consciousness is the cutting edge of soul work on the planet. Relatively few souls have emerged on that horizon. The most likely tribes at that level are relationships between two Stage Five souls. Stage Five souls have an intimate understanding of the connection of all that exists and the dependence they have on a larger community for the basic necessities of life. The communities that support this level of soul work are yet to be created.

The question remains. How do Stage Four and Five tribal communities emerge? They emerge as souls emerge from Stage Two and Three tribes. New forms emerge from a model. Without a model, a formative idea, no new form can come into being. All new forms in the universe emerge from a field of intelligence that contains the virtual form that guides the growth of the manifest form.

The idea and vision come first. Souls contain the model for the body that will awaken into partnership with a soul. And souls bring the model for the communities that will support their own evolution. These souls will have to create their own new tribal community.

5

SLEEPING SOULS, SLEEPING TRIBES

Sleeping Souls

WHAT DOES IT MEAN for souls to go to sleep, to slumber, or forget who they are, in a way that is characteristic of what I have called Stage Two?

Imagine the sunlight coming into a tree. The intense fire of the sun emits photons. These photons are absorbed into the tree's leaves by the process of photosynthesis. In this way, the photon energy is converted into the dense structure of the tree, including leaves, bark, wood, and oxygen.

As Thom Hartmann points out in his brilliant book *The Last Hours of Ancient Sunlight,* plants are made mostly of air and sunlight, not primarily of soil elements as is commonly believed. Almost all life is dependent in one way or another upon the light of the sun as a primary source of energy for this structure-building and oxygen production process.

When the wood of the tree is touched with fire, the embedded photon energy is transformed once more into heat and light, returning to something that resembled its original state, but now within the framework of matter. Until that combustion takes place, the photon energy of the sun has been hidden within the form of the tree, animating and expanding a design structure inherent in the seed of the tree.

In this way, the sun's photons work to build up and support the structure of the matter into which they have been absorbed, but this occurs beneath the surface where the operation is hidden from view. For photons to become a creative force at the level of the density of matter, they have to merge with matter until they can re-emerge into a form that is a reflection of their original nature. We recognize that original nature by the emergence of light in the form of fire.

One can think of the soul in the same way. The soul, like light, is a wave form—a field of energy. The soul field is encoded with the information that defines the unique qualities of a particular soul, including the secrets of its fate and destiny. Entering into its assigned body, it works in relation to a design structure in the DNA, which is the continually adapting seed from which the body grows into the particular form that we recognize as a human body.

As the soul enters the embryonic seed of the body, it disappears from sight. It works beneath the surface. While the body is developing and growing, the hidden soul imparts its energy and design information to the body and its temporary organizing consciousness, the personality. Like the photons of sunlight, the soul subordinates itself to the service of the growth and evolution of the form of matter into which it has entered.

As the body matures, it provides the platform for the direct expression of the soul's nature, just as a mature tree fulfills its purpose by providing shade, fruit, a home for other living beings, and the wood that is used in construction, as well as the heat and light that arise from its combustion.

Just as a tree becomes ignited with fire, the body must be ignited with the soul's purpose before the soul's destiny catches on fire, becoming visible as the passion that we can all recognize. When someone's soul catches fire, we can all see it—in the fire in their eyes, in the light in their faces, and in the brightness of their auras.

Wood's potential fire is ignited from outside by lightning or a match. Souls "sleeping" within the body are ignited into awakening from the outside as well. What sets fire to the soul and brings it back to the remembrance that it is a soul is the experience of unconditional love.

What makes the soul ever so receptive to this love is the pain that souls experience if they are not expressing themselves when the body has matured into a sufficient platform for that expression. There is a time for the soul to emerge, and we experience the absence of that emergence in some form such as illness, depression, emotional suffocation, or other attention-grabbing signals. In the tree, it is the dryness of the wood that makes it receptive to the combustion of fire. When we feel dryness in our lives, our souls are ready to ignite and release their light into the world.

But there the analogy ends. There is a critical difference between trees and humans. Plants and animals go through a predictable and inevitable cycle of birth and death, in which there is no possibility of emergence into a creative, evolving state. What distinguishes humans from all other life on the planet is that we are designed to evolve within the frame of a single life. Our DNA is a continually evolving seed form.

What humans share with plants and animals is the initial subordination of light to the development of the body. In both there is *devolution* of light into a dense form from which light eventually re-emerges.

What distinguishes humans is that the emergence of that light signals not a *dissolution* of the form, but an *empowerment* of the form with the soul purpose that leads to a unique destiny unavailable to plants and animals. While that soul purpose depends both on the body's form and on its emergence from it, it also depends on the *freedom* to evolve. Of all the kingdoms of matter, only humans can achieve freedom, and only humans depend on freedom for their growth.

Even when a soul has emerged into self-awareness, it cannot be free without some level of support from its tribe. The principal distinction between Stage Two tribes and tribes of more evolved consciousness is the existence of both a context of freedom and those processes that teach an emerging soul how to access and use the freedom that souls need to evolve into their destiny. [For readers who are interested in a more technical description of the process of devolution of light into matter and the evolution of light through kingdoms of matter we know as plants, animals and humans, along with an analysis of the unique quality of freedom that emerges at the stage of evolution represented by the human kingdom, I would suggest reading Arthur M. Young's *The Reflexive Universe: Evolution of Consciousness,* Robert Briggs Associations 1976.]

Sleeping Tribes

Just as the soul's forgetfulness of its own identity is analogous to the process by which light disappears into a developing tree, there is also an analogy between sleeping members of a tribe and the unconscious tribe into which they are born.

Just as the soul initially subordinates its identity to the development of the physical body in order to lend design information for the creation of the necessary physical platform for its work, a tribal member's early participation in the life of the tribe serves to subordinate its own ultimate destiny by lending its energy to the development of the tribe upon which it depends for survival. Only when the tribe is mature enough to assure group survival can it provide for individual freedoms. And only then can a member soul learn to use that freedom in the process of its own emergence. In this way, a soul must serve tribe first, and itself second, because the soul cannot survive without the tribe.

The same is true across the span of human evolution as a whole, during which humans have searched for a form of community that not only serves the survival of the race, but the "thrival" of humans at the level of soul evolution.

The process of tribes reaching beyond mere survival has moved forward in fits and starts. The memes of individual freedom and democracy have emerged into political forms in recent centuries, but have not taken firm hold yet for the simple reason that there is not a critical mass of humans with the skills of consciousness necessary to manifest those ideals in practice. Those concepts have been corrupted and coopted by greater numbers of humans of lesser consciousness. The United States perhaps represents the best example of that.

If a critical mass of humans has not evolved to a point that the collective tribal consciousness can support individual soul freedom, then the awakening soul's subordination to the development and viability of the tribe may no longer serve either the tribe or the individual soul. At that point, the soul has to choose to continue to subordinate by working to change the tribe, or leave the tribe. Nevertheless, humans depend on *some* tribe to survive just as a soul depends on a body, even a broken one, for its connection to the earth. When a soul moves away from the original, large tribe, it still needs to assure viability. It needs another community.

At this time in human history, Stage Three souls—the souls that know that they are souls—remain in Stage Two communities even as they form small Stage Three communities within the larger Stage Two communities. It is becoming increasingly apparent, however, that Stage Two nation-tribes are not only failing, but are likely to destroy the human relationship with the earth in the process. The first unanswered question is whether smaller communities *can* form that are viable and still remain within those failing Stage Two communities. The second is whether tiny soul tribes that might operate at Stage Three, Four, and Five can form and survive *anywhere* without a dependence upon the failing Stage Two tribes.

Sri Aurobindo, a twentieth-century Indian freedom fighter and spiritual writer, suggested perhaps a hundred years ago that the rational mind has turned human attention to the external world to such a degree that the insufficiently developed soul cannot pull the attention to itself. He argued that the rational mind, left to itself, will destroy humankind, and that only a development of a mature soul consciousness can balance the mind's nature and empower its potential.

The counterbalance to this mind that we now know as the patriarchy is the presence of the soul in the heart field within the frame of the human body. Sri Aurobindo wrote at great length about the importance of bringing attention to the soul, bringing the soul within the heart, bringing the personality within the control of the soul, and bringing the body into service of the soul's agenda. That heart-grounded soul, then, is the counterbalance to the patriarchy, and it is the very key to the emergence of an energized and powerful feminine, one that has the capacity to call the unbalanced masculine into a new dynamic balance *and* partnership with the feminine.

In the unconscious mind of patriarchal communities, it is ever so clear that the individual exists only to serve the survival of the community in the way determined by a powerful but unconscious class of humans who control the political and economic nature of the tribe. The culture of these communities, whether it is based in the myth of a king's divine right or the myth of a president's democratic mandate, has historically served to keep individuals disempowered.

An individual breaking with the conventional thinking and behavior that characterizes the culture of these communities has risked imprisonment, banishment, ostracism, or death. Despite some real differences in practice, this is as true in the United States as in nations that do not claim the enlightened posture of democracy.

In the past, the collective global patriarchy did not have the power to destroy the planet, despite its ability to spread across the entirety of the world. Those patriarchies enslaved, tortured, and dominated in the same way as still occurs, but with much less efficiency. Now, however, the new corporate-flavored, high-tech, global patriarchy is not so limited. It can manipulate not only how nations go to war, but the distribution of energy, food, and water at a global level, and it does so without concern for the cost of human health and life. It can put human survival as a whole at risk, and it is rapidly doing so.

The real challenge arises from the momentum of the dominant culture. I see that culture of "developed" countries like a high-speed train racing along parallel rails. The rails that determine the train's direction and destination are formed of two toxic and parallel forces.

On one rail we find the body politic made up of governments managed by the corporations that seek to strip people and the earth of wealth by any means necessary, in the name of neoliberal capitalism. On the other rail we find the priestly chorus of neoclassical economists who offer divine legitimacy to any government that will embrace like holy commandments the dogma of free markets, monetization, progress, and infinite growth. One rail is made of false prophets, and the other of false profits.

The patriarchal engineer of this train is unfortunately the pinnacle of human evolution stuck in an early stage: an unbridled masculine force of cosmic dimension that has yet to find its balance on a feminine planet. Our beautiful brains have not yet been mated with our hearts, nor our infinite souls with our beautiful bodies—the next necessary evolutionary steps if humans are to survive. In the meantime, the immature masculine force, dangerous throughout human history, has now fashioned from technology and fossil fuels a train that runs with such speed and force that it will not be stopped unless it jumps the tracks or runs out of fuel.

Behind the powerful engines of this train are passenger cars of all description, from the luxury models to boxcars. If the train crashes, neither the wealthy nor the more "conscious" among us will be exempt. Ecological disaster on the planet will be the great leveler.

Not to belabor the metaphor, but to take it just one step further, it is not surprising that passengers on the train cannot see what lies ahead. Almost all of us are in the cars behind the engine. Our view is limited to the scene passing rapidly by, which feels to most of us ever so much like progress, even if the speed of change we experience is a little disconcerting.

If a few of us are heading to the back of the train with the intention of disconnecting a few cars, it is in the hope that we can preserve something to enable another generation of humans to begin anew. It is in the hope that there are places Monsanto has not reached, that there are places where there is still good water, and that there are places where people know how to grow food.

Even if there are heroes of legend who can fight their way to the cab of the train and throw out the engineers of doom, the likelihood is that this movie will not end with the train stopped in time for the crash to be averted. The persistent patriarchy that has held the planet in its grip for so long has reached a tipping point. The growth model and the human and environmental violence upon which it depends are clearly unsustainable. The likelihood of a new political system replacing the old with a new consciousness that has the skill to lay down the tracks of a different nature is not high. So our ability to dream an alternative future is all the more important.

Humans have an as yet untapped capacity to *know* how to go forward and to *act* in accordance with those knowings, two qualities that represent a balance of our feminine and masculine natures. On the other hand, unless humans find a balanced, sustainable relationship between the highest qualities of the feminine and the masculine, both within themselves and between themselves and the earth, this opportunity for humans to advance the evolution of consciousness will sadly end, and end sadly. On the third hand, if even some humans are successful in creating that more balanced and conscious relationship, then the beautiful advances in human evolution that have preceded this time can provide the foundation for a developing consciousness that is more intentional, skillful, sustainable, and potent.

As it becomes apparent that these old tribal structures in modern form are indifferent to the circumstance or life of the individual soul, awakening souls are faced with critical questions. Do we fight to reform the old, or do we create the new? Do we create solutions other than trying to treat the dying body of the old by protesting and pushing for reforms that will not be enacted by indifferent politicians? These are difficult questions.

It is a dilemma that Zera too found herself facing. Do we

spend our energy protesting the megalith? Do we stand in front of the tank, or the train? Do we take up arms? Or do we find each other and create alternative tribes where the stand we may have to take is for an alternative that we have already put into motion?

As human consciousness has evolved against the dangerous trends of modern culture, we continue to think in terms of new and sustainable communities. But new models of community have not emerged that displace the model of the old. Sustainability for the sake of survival of the human tribe is an ethic that falls short of our purpose and could be created within the patriarchy, were it just a bit more awake. However, sustainability for the sake of a soul evolution that contemplates a co-active and co-creative partnership with the body and the earth is an entirely different model.

So, while this notion of soul tribes and tambos is not a complete flip of the notion of sustainable and intentional community that continues to find its footing, it does represent a soul perspective that gives a different emphasis and purpose to the work of inventing new communities. Humans still need community to survive, but community must exist ultimately to serve the individual, in light of one critical fact: evolution of consciousness proceeds one human soul at a time. It does not occur by the mere continuity of communities made up of one generation of humans substituting themselves for the prior generation with a slightly increased standard of living. We have yet to discover the way of living that is necessary both for human survival and the evolution of consciousness. The process of balancing the feminine and masculine at the level of evolution that humans represent must occur within individuals. The mechanism of community must no longer be control, but freedom and soul skill development.

This freedom is not the freedom of anarchy, but the freedom that arises from the cultivation of a shared responsibility for the mutual task of individual soul actualization. This notion of individual freedom and its relation to individual responsibility has long been a recognized political aspiration, as reflected in foundational documents that underwrite the express but as yet unrealized goal of nominally democratic societies.

We know that a democracy cannot exist without its members having the skills necessary to support the assumption of personal responsibility. The longstanding assumption is that universal education is the basis for providing those skills. Yet our educational systems have failed in those goals, in part for the want of a greater understanding that freedom is the foundation not only of a political freedom that includes spiritual and religious freedoms, but of the evolution of consciousness itself.

The freedom that supports evolution demands an individual skill set that extends far beyond the ability to regurgitate information, to learn the skills and disposition for consuming, or to do critical thinking. It demands the realization by a critical mass of individuals of their respective soul destinies, one human soul at a time. It demands a new skill set—including the skill of controlling our own attention, placing that attention in our own hearts, and connecting soul to body, self to other, humans to earth and heaven, and heaven to earth.

This a matter not merely of *political* concern, but of *spiritual* concern, which is about humans becoming partners in the creation of the cosmos. So long as politics is not concerned with empowering souls, then politics itself can have no soul, which is where the United States finds itself in this moment.

In the blink of evolutionary time that human existence represents, humans might appear to have accomplished much, but our human role in the larger process of the evolution of consciousness has only begun. The potential of our role is far richer than what we have accomplished or can imagine. Our creative capacities have shown themselves in a variety of ways, but our extraordinary ventures in science, medicine, technology, art, literature, and music have been so coopted and distorted by commercial exploitation that these advances also threaten to cut short our opportunities for evolution. In the greater scheme of things, it might not be so important that humans fail their potential, were it not for one important point: the evolution of consciousness as a whole seems to depend on humans meeting their potential.

There is more at stake than our own survival, comfort, and

entertainment. Humans represent a linchpin in the relationship between the subtle heaven realms and the dense earth realms, a connection that is essential to the fuller expression of the infinite intelligence of the universe in the dense structure of matter. It is no coincidence that all humans seek the experience of connection. That seeking is the very impulse to become what humans have the potential to be, which is the very connection between heaven and earth.

Humans are the bridge between the infinite fields of cosmic intelligence and the purposeful, intentional actions that manifest that intelligence in an unfoldment of creation at the level of matter. Humans *are* the very connection that they seek, if only they can awaken to who they are and what their role in the evolution of consciousness can be.

For that to occur, humans have to figure out, one at a time, what that purpose is and how to be on the planet in a sustainable way that provides the long time it will take to fulfill that purpose. Only by humans becoming the connection between heaven and earth can the play of consciousness reach its potential, which is to unfold and reveal heaven's love in the realm of matter in the process of creation.

Once formed, a tribe is likely to remain in the consciousness that formed it. It seems to me that new tribes form because individuals leave old tribes and express the uniqueness of their own consciousness into a new form that is shared with other individuals whose consciousness is operative at the same level.

This distinction is important because it suggests something about the strategy that individuals might take relative to the tribe in which they are uncomfortable. If we understand that the tribe can't change without a sufficient number of individual souls evolving to the next level, and if we understand something of how individuals change, we are confronted with a choice.

If we sense that our own individual evolution has exceeded the average in a way that allows us to see a more enlightened way for the tribe to function, we can become activists with the object of improving the level at which the tribe itself operates. That possibility is consistent with the assumption upon which modern democratic theory rests.

We have the option of both evolving ourselves, and becoming an activist in the process by which the tribe itself might change in some incremental way. Alternatively, we might choose an activism that departs a tribe in order to form another. There is a time when we stop *arguing* for difference, and move on to *being* that difference. To save our souls, and the work of consciousness that our souls represent, we may need to move on to another tribe.

6

CHOOSING WHERE THE SOUL WILL WORK

EVOLVING SOULS ARE FREE to choose to do their work within the tribe in which they first find themselves, or to leave it in search of another. However, moving to a new tribe is not a necessary condition for soul evolution. On the contrary, the conscious choice to remain in the discomfort of being in a Stage Two tribe can easily provide the grist that grinds the hard seed of a soul's fate into the flour of destiny.

Throughout history, souls have worked in this way, staying to face the challenges of their particular fate, transcending which they create the opportunity to manifest their unique destiny. Whether leaving is essential for a particular soul is a question only the soul can answer, by looking at all possibilities through the lens of the heart.

Leaving is not about avoiding discomfort, although the personality uninformed by a mature soul might think so. Discomfort will likely await our arrival at another destination. The experience of discomfort in our tribe of origin or elsewhere is either a gift of fate or the challenge creation itself represents. It is discomfort or outright pain that prods the sleeping soul both to awaken and to continue forward in the process of soul evolution and the work of creation.

When an awakening soul leaves a tribe in response to discomfort, the decision may arise from an unexamined projection that the discomfort is the fault of the tribe, rather than the hand of fate working to awaken the soul so it can enlighten a projecting personality. On the other hand, leaving a tribe that has given rise to discomfort may reflect the soul's accurate assessment that its work of fate is completed, and that the tribe no longer supports the work of destiny. The women whose stories I told in Chapter Two were in the process of making this kind of decision. They were deciding whether their work involved changing an old tribe and whether another tribe might better support their souls' work.

Souls emerging self-aware into their own destinies will likely find themselves in one of two very general groups. One group will emerge into an activism directed toward changing the tribe around them. These souls will work in the tribe of discomfort and bring their gifts to the process of changing that community into a more conscious, soul-supportive home. A second group will emerge into a different activism I alluded to earlier in the Preface that involves a focus upon *receiving, embodying, protecting, evolving, recording, and translating the process knowledge* that represents the accumulated wisdom of how souls evolve in collaboration with heaven and earth. Both of these groups are dependent upon each other to do their respective work. Both are equally important.

Peruvian tradition has called these souls chakaruna. Both groups act as bridges for the work that heaven seeks to do with earth as its partner. The skill set that underlies their unique individual gifts is the same. This skill set is *attentional*. It includes learning how to control attention, how to restore attention to the field of the soul, how to anchor that soul attention in the field of the heart, and how to move it among the infinity of other-dimensional fields that inform the soul's work. The soul will find the answer that informs its work through the lens of the heart, which connects the soul's attention to the guidance that those other-dimensional fields offer.

New soul tribe communities—tambos—can support both groups in their emergence. Some souls will visit the new tambos and return to their tribal communities of origin to create sub-tribes of greater consciousness within those tribes of origin. Others might remain for a longer time in those places where the new tribes form to create the new home for cultivation and preservation of the process knowledge.

The decision to leave the tribe of original discomfort will turn, for the maturing soul, on the nature of that particular soul's destiny. "Is my work to remain and work here, in my old tribe, or to move on to another?" This is the crux of the question that will define how emerging souls make their way home.

These are not abstract decisions. The soul has to take a position. Long before my soul awakened to a sense of *I am,* I experienced discomfort in my own small rural community in the United States and found myself working to change it. That work involved the ordinary kinds of public service that volunteers do in Chambers of Commerce, by supporting political candidates, by organizing opposition to corporate action that might endanger the environment in the region, and by supporting cultural events that might enrich the life of all small communities.

I helped, for example, to form a nonprofit organization that worked to restore a 1915 opera house into a multi-use facility, which helped the community attract a theatrical producer whose presence enriched the cultural life of the area. My service on a statewide higher education regulating commission led to my forming another nonprofit organization that created a unique distance educational infrastructure for place-bound adults. This fifteen-year effort resulted in dozens of people receiving higher educational degrees that they would not have otherwise obtained, benefitting both themselves and other small communities in our area.

I also coordinated a small group that successfully opposed the creation of a nuclear waste dump near our community. More recently, I worked with another small group that successfully opposed a natural gas fracking operation that proposed to drill atop our community's watershed.

I have little doubt that my work benefitted the community, even though I often found myself frustrated. In retrospect, I can see that my own unconscious personality often projected the source of my discomfort upon the community in which I worked. On the one hand, it felt natural to perform some public service. On the other, that motivation was infected by an unconscious perception that I would be happier if my surroundings were different. What I didn't understand is that my personality remained unaware of the presence of a soul that was signaling its own discomfort with the trajectory of my life in general. From a soul perspective, the experience of those years in that community was grooming my soul with experience for an altogether different kind of work.

In time, I found myself with dual perceptions. As my own soul emerged into view, and as my soul learned to perceive the world through the lens of the heart, I found myself drawn to the work that emerged for me in Peru. Because I have been pulled to this work and place by soul and heart, it matters little what perception I might have of the tribes—nation, college, high school, various communities of residence, family—that I am required to leave behind. No critique is necessary. I have had to leave because my soul work is elsewhere.

My mind, on the other hand, created a narrative to explain my leaving that is quite different from the storyline that reports on the impulse of my heart. Almost three decades into my work in supporting candidates for office at the state and national levels, I concluded that politics had become so coopted by the financial influence of national and global corporations that my involvement no longer made any difference for my small community.

I concluded that corporations had succeeded in taking control of the common consciousness of the American public through television, technology, processed foods, and pharmaceuticals. The same corporations took control of politicians and, through them, also took control at the national and state levels of economic, financial, domestic, and foreign policy. I saw little possibility of meaningful Congressional or grassroots action on health, mental health, violence, overpopulation, health care systems, climate change, food production, or wealth distribution.

I observed the trajectory of neoliberal capitalism in a larger frame of both time and global economics. I concluded that the United States was not only a nation in decline, but that its decline, and its many causes, made my further participation largely futile. My mind was made up, concluding that it was time to follow the soul's independent decision.

One job of the rational mind is to rationalize. For me, that mental story rationalized the soul's independent, heart-based decision to leave, and that story arose over time. When my heart's knowing arose, it was instantaneous. It took my mind longer to find reason in the heart's simple knowing that it was time to leave without regard for this negative perception of cultural decline. Moving from judgment to discernment allowed the mind to embrace the heart's perspective without the fear that drives judgments. Body and soul were of one mind, more or less, and they embarked on a quest for a new tribe. And all of that seemed right, even if the mind's constructed understanding was neither complete nor accurate. What was true for me was the heart's own knowing, without regard for any understanding. I make no claim that my mind's understanding is accurate, and I try to keep my mind open to other possibilities as time passes.

The analysis my mind had made about my tribe of origin might have done just the opposite for a soul whose destiny would be different. The challenges I observed in my culture evoked an underlying soul nature that perceived the need to preserve and develop human understanding of the evolution of consciousness against the possibility of human disaster. Those same challenges might evoke another soul's decision to stay in order to blunt and turn away the evident danger. Both are critically important, and each soul must feel into its own pathway.

And those pathways continue to turn. As I have come to the end of the process of writing this book, my heart is bringing me back to my nation-tribe of origin, to continue my work here in the United States, with continuing ties to the spiritual traditions of Peru that are looking to us as partners in this continuing work. My mind, in the meantime, continues its work of understanding where the heart is leading.

7

PLANT SHAMANS AND PACOS: COMPLEMENTARY TRADITIONS

TOURISTS VISITING Peru's world-famous Machu Picchu will arrive first in Cusco, the ancient capital of the Inca. Linking Cusco to Machu Picchu is Peru's Sacred Valley. Dr. Ruben Orellana, a respected Peruvian archeologist, told me that "Sacred Valley" is a name assigned the Vilcanota River valley not by Peru's indigenous population, but by Peru's tourist marketing industry.

The commodity increasingly marketed for sale is "healing." Healing, like the notion of "indigenous," is a big tent, and all that is spiritually Peruvian gets thrown into it.

Among Peru's many spiritual traditions with their own regional flavors, there are two predominant forms. Amazonian jungle healers work with plants, rattles, drums, whistling, song, and prayer. Ayahuasca is the preeminent plant in this tradition. It is said to be the "mother" of all the other plants in the Amazonian shamanic pharmacy.

The mountain healing tradition represented by the Q'ero of Incan ancestry employs various prayer forms and initiations powered by portable altars called mesas. A mesa is a collection of sacred objects, including stones called *kuyas* that represent energetic connections to various spirit helpers. Foremost among those helpers are the mountain spirits I've already mentioned, known as apus. These sacred objects are wrapped in a rectangular textile called a mestana. Westerners initiated in this tradition call themselves mesa carriers. Q'ero use bells, but do not use rattles, drums, plants, or voice as healing tools.

Spiritual tourists routinely find these two healing traditions mingling at the middle elevation between the mountains and the jungle in the region of the Sacred Valley, which drops from about 9,700 feet (2,956 meters) at Pisac to about 6,700 feet (2,042 meters) at Aguas Calientes. The Q'ero have come down to the Valley from much higher elevations in the mountains, while the ayahuasqueros have come up from near-sea-level jungle.

Although tourists may seek out these traditions in their respective habitats, both traditions are also seeking out the tourists. The Sacred Valley and Cusco provide a larger audience for these traditions, and both traditions have now taken their show on the road to the U.S. and Europe.

The ceremonies conducted by these respective traditions look very different from each other. If one were to ask the object of these traditional practices, the common answer would be translated into English as "healing." Similarly, one commonly hears that both traditions are "shamanic." My own teachers have said or assumed as much. And that had been my understanding since my second trip to Peru in 2002.

So I was recently more than a little surprised when Q'ero elder Don Umberto said otherwise. I spent two days in ceremony with him in California in 2013. His translator said that the Q'ero are mystics, not shamans. He says that the Q'ero mystics should be called pacos, and that paco does not equate with shaman even though "shaman" is the term into which we tend to throw all indigenous healing practitioners.

The implication is significant. Both mystics and shamans are concerned with healing, to be sure. However, Umberto's translator emphasized two points. First, he said, the Q'ero are working with the higher vibrations represented by the apus and "unity consciousness." Second, the Q'ero do not work with plant medicines, trance states, drums, rattles, voice, song, whistling, or sound other than bells. That list characterizes, the translator said, what shamans do.

Shamanism is often defined to include the use of trance states in which the shaman journeys to other dimensions, whether the trance is induced by plant medicines, sound, a focus of concentration and intention, or otherwise. While trance states can and do touch into higher dimensions, the work of shamans seems to me to be focused more directly on the body and the healing of its dysfunctions. Drums, rattles, and singing—whatever else they represent—are themselves lower vibration tools.

In my own lexicon, the higher vibrations speak to the soul and lure it from its unconscious enmeshment with the body, which is an aspect of healing, but one that addresses soul more than body. My sense is that mystics ascend with their souls to the higher vibrations to focus and concentrate the soul, while shamans work to clear out the dysfunctional patterns that prevent the soul from partnering with the body and assuming its full power in the world.

These two practices are not mutually exclusive, and there is an inherent overlap in them. My perspective, which focuses on the soul, suggests that mystics work with the body to support the work of the soul, while shamans work with the soul to support the work of the body. I think the distinction is important and that categorizing both traditions with the same general label of shamanism blurs an important difference.

Don Umberto points out that the distinctly different geographies of these two traditions also reflect an essential difference between them. Umberto points to elevation itself as significant. As the Q'ero characterize the difference, the mountain elevations above 12,000 feet (3,600 meters) represent the upper world of indigenous cosmology with its higher frequencies, while the jungle, below an elevation of 3,500 feet (1,067 meters), represents the lower world with its slower frequencies of density. Some, though not all, of the Q'ero live above 12,000 feet. The upper world, Umberto says, allows a direct experience of *sami,* the pure and tangible energy that we associate with the unconditional love of the cosmos. At lower elevations, he says, the denser fields of energy interfere with our ability to experience that energy.

Amidst the modern assemblage of "shamanic" teaching programs created for Western consumption, the average spiritual tourist may not catch the central distinction made by Don Umberto between the traditions of pacos and plant shamans. Peru has marketed itself as the land of the Inca to a Western audience for whom shamanism is now the spiritual rage. The Q'ero, regarded as the direct descendants of the Inca and the safe-keepers of that tradition, are a centerpiece of Peru's attraction. The fact that the Q'ero see themselves as a mystical rather than shamanic culture might cause some Western teachers not to emphasize this distinction even if they catch it, since it could complicate a necessarily simple marketing message that sees the burgeoning interest in shamanism as the hook.

Both traditions have deep roots. For the Westerner who is sampling these traditions, the distinctions may make little difference. But for those who are on a soul quest, determined to make good use of the fading opportunities offered by ancient traditions, the difference is important. It is not a question whether one tradition is more powerful than another. It is, instead, a matter of understanding the power of each, and how each serves a particular purpose at different stages of soul evolution.

While Don Umberto's remarks underlined the essential difference between these traditions, it evoked something quite deeper in my own mind. In light of my focus on a soul perspective, the vision of mystical and shamanic practices working side by side implied a beautifully powerful complementarity. That complementarity provides a key to unlocking some of the mystery of the rich spiritual teachings that are emerging for Westerners in Peru, as well as a foundational understanding for the creation of soul tribes.

In *The Soul's Critical Path*, I described how the soul typically, though not inevitably, forgets its soul nature upon the entry into a human body. The divine scheme that has injected souls deep into the heart of matter has devised the oft-painful challenges of fate as the means by which souls are offered the opportunity to recover the memory that they *are* souls. When souls learn to engage fate with gratitude for the lessons contained within its challenges, then fate begins to give way to the destiny that can be created from a soul's special gifts.

The recovery of a soul's memory that it is a unique and infinite field of energy quite distinct from the body/mind/personality complex is facilitated by experiences in which the human personality feels connected to everything. When ordinary, personality-based human consciousness can taste something akin to that unity consciousness, it can leave for the moment its ordinary experience of loneliness and separation. That taste of unity consciousness replaces a sense of separation with an irrefutable sense of connection. This taste of unity is the gold that Eastern mysticism seeks through the practice of meditation.

My recent visit with Don Umberto led me to understand that the experience of unity consciousness is also a primary goal of Q'ero initiations. I think this is part of what Umberto implies by his identification of his tradition with mysticism rather than shamanism.

It is the soul that tastes the sense of connection that is what unity consciousness feels like in the body. It is the soul's consciousness that both lends consciousness to the body and makes it possible for the body to have a sense of feeling loved and safe. That sense opens the body to a far deeper level of healing work than can otherwise occur.

The taste of unity consciousness and the consequent relaxation of the body's defenses represent a critical threshold that sets the stage for a grander adventure. That adventure is found in the opportunity to bring the creative aspirations of heaven directly into an engagement with matter in order to further the open-ended process of manifesting Love in the realm of form.

When the soul remembers that it is not only connected to the Divine, but that the soul itself is one way in which the Divine makes an appearance in time, then the soul is in the unique position of bringing great leverage to the challenges faced by the human personality here on planet earth. Those challenges teach the soul skills necessary for the emergence of the soul's creative gifts.

In Western culture, we recognize that the body carries the wounding of childhood trauma. The notion of reincarnation suggests that this wounding runs even deeper than our childhood experiences, holding that the body of today carries the memory of woundings that go back for the thousands of yesterdays that reincarnating souls live. This memory, for each of us, probably includes many episodes of violence in which we have experienced being a victim at some times and a perpetrator at others.

Beyond our personal soul experience of many lifetimes, the DNA of each human may include the memory of all violence experienced by humans in general. I have certainly found both in the visions of my own soul history. When I have touched into the ocean of sadness that attends human experience, for example, I know that it is not all mine. As I experience patriarchy in myself, I find also the thread to the patriarchy as a whole. And I find in my own memory the experience of the feminine as well, a memory that connects me to the experience of the feminine as a whole. While the conscious mind cannot hope to understand the full implication of these experiences, it is important for each soul to taste as much as possible, both to remember itself and to discover the potential of its own future trajectory.

A central question for the soul is how to help the body release the wounding represented by this historical imprint. Without both such a release and the recovery of a sensitized perception of the painful rigor of human experience over time, the body cannot partner with an awakened soul that is ready to engage its destiny as a co-creator.

This question arises as a soul begins to experience the awakenings that signal its forward movement on its evolutionary journey. If the soul's attention is drawn toward the Peruvian milieu, a more specific question arises: do I seek out the plants or the pacos—the shamans or the mystics?

In *The Soul's Critical Path,* I suggested that it is not an either/or proposition. Before the soul can begin the process of helping the body to heal its deep trauma, it must distinguish itself from the body and capture at least a taste of unity consciousness. From that platform, the soul can share the Love emanating from heaven and earth with the body, bringing the body to an experience of feeling loved and safe. With the body coming to the opening that a sense of love and safety facilitates, then the traumas of past life and lives can be more easily accessed and released.

So there is a sequence that attends the evolution of the soul. First comes the pain that humans inevitably encounter. Some of us, by learning to control our attention with some technique of meditation, are able to transmute pain into soul awakenings. From awakenings, we have the opportunity to find our way to the unity experience. In this experience, we can recover the memory that we are indeed souls, and that we are of Divine origin.

With that memory recovered, the personality can begin to yield its fearful ego identity to the soul. With that shift of personal identity, the soul can assume control over the beleaguered personality that was not designed to do the heavy lifting of healing the body's traumas. This is a way of talking about the process of surrendering our "self" to our "Self," a way of speaking that makes so little sense until we see that Self and soul are one and the same, while self is another way of speaking of the personality. In my own way of talking about this, both Self and soul remain absolutely unique and individually encoded for particular work on the planet. Soulness is not a state of dissolution within an infinite Divine, but an individualized expression of it with access to the resources of the Divine when the soul is able to remember who it is and focus itself.

By helping the body and its personality feel loved and safe, the soul creates the necessary condition for the body to release the crippling fear that has given rise to defensive and aggressive patterns of behavior. These patterns have denied the soul its physical vehicle in the world of matter. With a soul perspective that uses multi-dimensional consciousness to access the many spirit helpers standing by with extraordinary means of healing, we can release the historical traumas that drive the unconscious motivations underlying our dysfunctional behaviors.

One tool for releasing the body's traumas and the associated behaviors is the engagement with the plant medicines. As I will discuss in more detail in the next chapter, the plant medicines represent a particularly powerful way of addressing those entrenched patterns quickly and effectively. We can access this healing help if we learn how to meet the medicines with skillful attention. That skillful attention arises from the soul remembering who it is and placing itself squarely within the frame of the body in the center of the field of the heart. From that position, the soul can share the Love emanating from heaven and earth. This is the primary gift of the integration of the experience of unity consciousness into a process of soul embodiment.

Once the body's fear can be held within the container of the soul's Love-light, and the dysfunctional defensive patterns are released, then the soul and body can partner for the adventure of consciousness that we know as creation, in which the higher frequencies of heaven can be harmonized with the lower vibrations of matter. This is the means by which creation expands into an infinite variety of forms.

The healing force of mysticism supports the emergence of the soul. The healing force of shamanism supports the clearing of the body's dysfunction. Each of these processes supports the other. Therein lies the complementarity of these two traditions.

So, how does that complementarity look in more detail?

8

THE Q'ERO PACOS: OUR SOULS ARE SOLAR

DURING MY RECENT visit with Don Umberto and Dona Bernadina, they performed karpay initiations and despacho ceremonies. Their translator said that the object of the initiations was "ascension." The despacho ceremonies were performed for the purpose, among others, of connecting our energy bodies to the apus, the mountain spirits.

The mountains, he said, exist in a fourth dimensional consciousness. On each of the two days of our time together, the despacho ceremony was performed first in order to enlist the powerful assistance of the apus in support of our ability to receive the karpay.

The karpay initiations were performed, the translator said, to create a connection with fifth dimensional consciousness. Throughout these ceremonies, the translator made reference to the soul in a way that appeared to assume, without saying it directly, that the participants should see themselves primarily as souls. Seeing oneself as a soul is what I have called a soul perspective, so long as it is an experiential event rather than a mere belief.

Although there are undoubtedly other effects intended by the pacos, one result of an initiation of the soul into a fifth dimensional experience is to invite the remembrance of oneself as a soul. The vibrational tuning these initiations represent is an invitation to the soul to emerge from its enmeshment in the body and to experience itself independent of the body—a being originating in a dimension other than the third dimension from which the body arises and to which it returns upon its death.

As I suggested in *The Soul's Critical Path*, this soul encounter with itself and its origin is preliminary to the experience of bringing the sense of love and safety to the body that facilitates the deepest of healings in the third dimensional body. For that reason alone, quite apart from any other soul work that the pacos might facilitate, I see the work with the Q'ero as preliminary to the work with the jungle plant shamans. The latter bring a different kind of work to bear on the soul's progress, as I will discuss below, even though the work of the plant shamans has the potential to strengthen the unity experience as well.

I hasten to add that I did not experience the work in Peru in the order I am proposing here. My own preliminary work with unity consciousness came from meditation in both Asian and Native American forms, particularly the intense meditative states achieved by vision questing in nature. However, I see that work as analogous to the work of the Q'ero. During these quests, my consciousness was connected to those upper realms, an experience evidenced by a state of bliss accompanied by my hearing Sanskrit mantras. I see this meditative practice as analogous to the practices of the Q'ero.

Like Tibetan mysticism, Q'ero spirituality is based in a relationship with the sun. The Q'ero see the light of the sun as the origin of everything in the third dimensional world of matter. The light of the sun, they say, is the manifestation of Love, and from Love everything emerges.

The Q'ero speak of our sun, the sun behind the sun, and the great sun behind all of that. That ultimate sun is the unity, and our experience of that sun is the experience of unity consciousness. We are also individuated suns, and that individuated sun is the soul.

The Q'ero see each human as a "little sun." In that way, we are all solar beings. Our souls are solar. Even before hearing the Q'ero solar cosmology, I experienced my own soul as a light as brilliant as the sun, shining from the center of my chest. So it was easy for me to resonate with this message.

Just as unity consciousness can be said to be the sun rising on the horizon of the soul, the soul itself can be seen as a sun that rises on the horizon of the body. The soul must first discover its own nature in the experience of unity's brilliant light, then it may shine upon the body, bringing the light of Love to the event horizon of the most fundamental layer of human matter, which resides in coding found in the DNA.

Ascension reveals the soul to itself in the experience of the unity consciousness. I suggested in *The Soul's Critical Path* that ascent is followed by a descent in which the soul moves consciously into the density of matter. Understood in this way, Peru offers complementary modalities that represent a fusion waiting to happen if the present cloud of confusion lifts just a bit.

Central to that confusion may be our understanding of healing. To speak of a huge subject very succinctly, I would say that mysticism uses its emphasis on higher frequencies to heal primarily by bringing the soul to experience both itself as a distinct entity and its unity with the whole of the Divine. Shamanism's engagement with the dense frequencies speaks more directly to the healing of the body and the release of the unconscious patterns that have arisen in response to historical wounding.

Strengthening the soul has immediate healing effects for the body as well, but does not complete that process. Conversely, strengthening the body has immediate effects for the ability of the soul to consolidate its position relative to the body, but does not itself bring the soul into its own wholeness.

Together, the two processes work more powerfully than either process working alone. Soul retrieval, for example, is a powerful shamanic process that works from the body perspective to arrange the return of a departed soul or soul part. A soul perspective might flip this process. If one works from a soul perspective, it would be possible to speak of the healing process as "body retrieval." Not all mystics work in this way, but those mystics of a tantric or vajrayana inclination that give importance to the soul's grounding in the body might fall into this category. I don't sense that the Q'ero are so concerned with body retrieval, and neither is the larger body of Asian mysticism. The complementarity that I am suggesting here is yet to be fully explored, but I see it as an approach pregnant with possibility for the process of grounding the soul in the body.

Just as the soul has to be awakened by the pain of the body, so must the potential of the body be awakened by the Love accessed by the soul. As the soul does not awaken without the Divine mechanism of fate, so the body does not receive this brilliant and fundamental Love-light of the cosmos in a manner sustainable over a lifetime without the soul's transmission of its solar nature to the body.

So it is not a matter of choosing between mysticism and shamanism, nor a matter of taking sides with either ascenders or descenders. Both are important. While we may go back and forth between the two as the souls inch forward in their evolution with the assistance of their bodies, we ultimately must ascend more fully into unity consciousness before we can descend more fully into the body and the larger realm of dense matter.

One particularly powerful tool for opening the body is the plant medicine, if the soul is drawn to using it.

9
THE ENTHEOGENIC PLANTS

I HAVE NEVER RECOMMENDED to anyone that they use plant medicines. What I do say is that plant medicines are a powerful agent for change, and that no one should engage with them unless he or she is ready to invite powerful change into one's life. Whether to use the plants is a question each person must answer for herself.

There is an important corollary to that suggestion. One who invites powerful change will do well to prepare for handling the changes that may come. One form of preparation is to have some idea of what the plants do and how they do it, although humans don't yet have a complete understanding of either.

My experience with the plants suggests they collaborate with the soul to speed the healing of the body's trauma. In retrospect, it feels to me that my meditative vision quests brought me to a soul awakening that opened me to an encounter with a plant shaman. That experience brought me to the Q'ero and a deeper engagement with my own soul work. In the process, my soul emerged into its own, and my soul brought me back to the plants to work further with the body's woundings. I didn't have a sense of the logic of this sequence while it was occurring, but a retrospective view from a soul perspective has given rise to the understanding that I am sharing here.

Can soul work with the body be done without the use of entheogenic plants? The answer is yes.

Without regard to the opportunities that plants might provide, the inherent momentum of a soul is to discover itself and its own unique nature, to explore dimensions beyond the body, to investigate the soul's relationship with the body, and to develop that very specific partnership with the body that will advance the evolution of consciousness in its specifically human quality. The fullness of this exploration arises in equal measure from grace and the skill of presence. Persistence, discipline, and humility will yield both grace and presence in time.

I have brought all of these qualities into my own explorations, sometimes more and often less. So, why use the plants? For me, the answer is that the plants have facilitated, amplified, and sped these explorations.

My experiences with meditation and vision questing started a process that made the soul more apparent to me, which is to say that it made the soul more apparent to itself. My subsequent encounter with ayahuasca brought my soul forward as a greater force within my personality. Because of the force of change that the ayahuasca introduced, I sought out a teacher of shamanism in the United States. My teacher taught his version of Q'ero tradition, calling it shamanism.

While my teacher did not address the difference between mysticism and shamanism, if he understood it, that preliminary study with him and with various other teachers provided a priceless context for my integration of these earlier experiences. This led to a self-recognition in my soul that has literally voiced itself as *I am*, leading to a shift of personal identity from the personality to the soul itself. From that threshold, I—as soul—could begin to address the issues of the body more directly.

In the Introduction, I spoke of three themes that arose as I reflected upon my plant experience: soul emergence, the search for home, and the acceleration of the pace of consciousness evolution and change in general. My own sense is that this particularly critical juncture in human history has given rise to an imperative that souls emerge into greater consciousness more quickly now.

My experience suggests that the plants serve to accelerate the speed at which the soul emerges from the body and the body releases dysfunctional adaptive patterns. Plants inform our understandings by mediating profound physical and visionary experiences that help to explain why we are experiencing pain in our lives and how the pain can be transmuted into soul growth—but only if we meet the plants halfway, which requires not inconsiderable skill on our part.

We must be able to meet the rigorous presentation of the plant experience with full attention, and we must learn how to integrate the information the plant experience provides and the change it offers. The plants do not, and cannot, do all of the work required for our personal transformations. Even if the plants perform physical, emotional, and psychological healings, we need to have the desire, will, and skill to fully manifest that work in our lives. The plants are not magic pills that cure without our full participation, but they can do something that I feel no pill can provide.

From a shamanic perspective, *all* plants play some role in the support of humans. But within the plant kingdom, there is a hierarchy. In the conversations that have attended my own plant experiences, I have continued to hear of the *master teaching plants.* These include a list of what often amounts to seven: ayahuasca, huachuma, tobacco, datura, psilocybin mushrooms, iboga, and peyote.

In addition, there are plants we call food, and others we call herbs. More recent research has begun to acknowledge the medicine and food value of what our culture has shunned as weeds or invasives. In addition, non-psychedelic mushrooms are coming to the attention of science not only as food, but also as medicine for the body and as a powerful force in the maintenance and restoration of our earth ecologies.

In the shamanic context, both the teacher plants and these other plants are regarded as falling into three categories, depending on the relationship they offer to us: *allies, totems, and messengers.*

Allies play a powerful role for a time during our lives, and a totem relationship is said to exist for a lifetime, while messengers come and go. Within these roles, some plants help us to better receive the master plants into our bodies and our consciousness, or to synergize with each other for particular healing effects.

So, plants play many supporting roles. They feed the body. They otherwise support the physical health by balancing, supporting, and curing its basic operations. Master teaching plants facilitate the emergence of soul, clear the defensive patterns that come to reside unconsciously in the body as a consequence of woundings, and open us to the possibility of communicating with other-dimensional fields of intelligence that await our attention. Expansive subjective evidence of this process exists in the written reports of people who have shared their ceremonial experiences with the plants, strongly supporting the idea that cosmic intelligence works in and through the master teaching plants.

My experience suggests that no psychology, no mental process, nor even a sensitive "mind/body" therapy, has the potential to move a person as quickly toward soul emergence and a soul/body partnership as an engagement with the master plants. That process is even quicker when a soul that is ready and willing can be supported with a program of preparation and integration leading to the development of soul skills that can collaborate with the medicine in service of healing the body.

I have to make an exception to this position. Near-death experiences also have the capacity to bring the soul into clear view. My own virtual near-death, described in detail in *The Soul's Critical Path,* allowed me to experience my soul as entirely distinct from my body. Near-death helps us distinguish what remains after death from what does not. It is not coincidental that the word ayahuasca is also translated as "vine of death." Death winnows the infinite from the finite. But there is for me an exception to the exception. My virtual near-death experience occurred in a process of psychodrama approximately three years after my initial encounter with ayahuasca. It is possible that the ayahuasca opened a door that let me taste death in this non-threatening way.

I suspect that the destiny of some of us may itself be intimately tied to the exploration of the plants and the dimensions to which they connect us. It may be the case that there are dimensions of consciousness that are not otherwise accessible. It may be that the exploration of one or more of the plants is a destiny in itself.

So, as with all soul questions, each of us must find the particular trajectory of our own path. The answer may involve an engagement with some of the entheogenic plants, or none at all. It is, finally, the most personal of questions, one that can be answered only at the level of individual soul inquiry with the body itself in the stillness of the heart field.

With that said, I want to share some observations on ayahuasca and huachuma arising from my own experience.

Ayahuasca

Ayahuasca is a bitter mix. Some recipes are easier to drink than others. For some people, the taste softens over time. My body invariably shudders as I swallow, and it shudders when I watch someone else drink it.

Early on in my experiences, the shudder was accompanied by some apprehension over what might follow. Over time, this anxiety subsided, but the shudder remained. My soul might think this is a good idea, but it is the body that carries the direct burden of the work. The body is quite capable of having its own opinion, as we know from its defensive reactions that arise automatically without regard for our consciousness intentions.

The bitterness itself seems to be associated with the means by which the medicine serves one of its primary purposes, which is to remove something from the body. The means of removal is, in part, throwing up. The purging most often clears whatever material the stomach holds, but it goes further than that.

For many people in their early stages of work, the purging continues beyond the act of clearing the stomach, sometimes for hours. The shamans say, directly or indirectly, that this prolonged purging is associated with clearing the habits that have held our bodies in persistent behaviors and our emotions in painful reactions.

If my ceremonies had stopped with the exhaustion that followed purging, I would have probably concluded that the sole purpose of the ayahuasca was to remove the dark detritus of historical woundings and defensive adaptations. But that was not the case.

The purging is frequently accompanied or followed by visions for which ayahuasca is also known. There are at least two kinds of visions, and I gave detailed examples of each in *The Soul's Critical Path.*

The first comes as the effects of the plant are first felt in the body. This one seems to stem from the direct interaction of the chemical nature of the plant with the chemicals of the brain. I call these the "plant" visions, attributing them to the direct action of the plant itself. For me, these visions are always colorful, dynamic patterns that elude description, even though I tried to describe them in that earlier book. No painting that I have ever seen captures the brilliant intensity of these visions.

The other kind of vision has been entirely different, no more or less dramatic, but filled with some combination of images, symbols, memories, vistas, voices, and words spoken or intuited in English. Some people experience and give voice to languages other than English, and possibly not earth-based at all. All of this latter visionary content amounts to *information.*

By calling the latter visions informational, I mean that they contributed a basis for creating *meaning* that helped me make sense of the process in which my life was involved. In turn, that meaning helped me to integrate these extraordinary experiences into changes that would make a difference in my life. But even when I could not elicit meaning, it has seemed that the informational experiences represented the visible aspect of work that was *re-patterning* my body and personality, replacing the less functional patterns that had just been removed.

This re-patterning has sometimes been described as analogous to downloading new software, or updating old software. As with my own computer, I sometimes need help with a repair, and I may not fully understand the software that gets downloaded for my use even as I am able to learn how to use it. More recently, I heard one young but experienced shaman of strong lineage speak in similar terms. He said that ayahuasca recodes the system of which body and soul are a part.

For me, the plant visions were initially fascinating but ultimately distracting as I began to anticipate the informational engagement that might but did not always follow. Yet the plant visions were mesmerizing, capturing the attention and tantalizing the mind to follow them deeper. If the attention were captured in this way, the attention might not be available to be present to the uprising of the informational experience.

I can appreciate that both forms of vision might be experienced as terrifying if there were no context that provided meaning to the experiences. It could feel as though control had been given up for a ride that could go anywhere. Because of this likely challenge, the shamans urge the participants to sit up and be present during the ceremony. For the same reason, I have come to see that the skill of paying attention and grounding that attention in the heart field is what transforms a ceremony from a terrifying ordeal into a blessed transmission of both healing and meaning.

So, the first job of the medicine is to clear out what doesn't work. The second is to replace what doesn't work with what does. Together, these two steps provide one way of describing what I mean when I refer to the notion of *healing*.

Healing is not an end in itself, but a step that precedes other and greater levels of change that can occur if we are able to integrate the healing. To integrate a healing means that we are able to capture the changes made by the medicine or healer so that the body and soul become sufficiently free of historical dysfunction to mature into a collaborative partnership in service of the ultimate work of the soul. This ultimate work is the work of destiny. The ability to integrate a healing is found most significantly in the skill of paying attention within the field of the heart. The mind's understandings will follow in time.

For me, it was the adoption of a soul perspective that gave sense and structure to the apparent chaos of the experience. I began to see myself as the soul, and it was the soul that was paying attention, focused within the field of the heart. With the soul perspective, the chaos of ceremony could distill more quickly into meaning, both during and after. And with that soul perspective, I could more easily open to the downloading of new software or codes that could serve a higher function of soul consciousness.

I found that my ceremonies transformed in such a way that simple exhaustion was only a passing experience. With the greater willingness and ability to surrender to the medicine that a soul perspective provided, I felt myself emerging through discrete and recognizable stages. Early exhaustion was followed by a certain emotional and energetic exhilaration, particularly if there was information I sensed to be meaningful or if I sensed that a healing of my body had occurred. Subtly different was a physical exhilaration, in which my body experienced a lift in strength and balance. I always felt stronger in the mornings after the ceremonies than in the afternoons before. In light of the rigor of the ceremonies, it felt paradoxical. But it always felt that a burden had been lifted, and that the purging had done its work.

In time, there was a sense of an ongoing process extending from ceremony to ceremony. There was one ceremony—described in detail in *The Soul's Critical Path*—in which I emerged through considerable rigor into what I felt to be the heart of the earth. I felt held in complete love. My body surrendered in that moment, feeling altogether safe. There were colors and images associated with the experience that have continued to repeat themselves in many, though not all, of the ceremonies that followed.

Unlike the colors often associated with chakras, the color that accompanied this extraordinary experience was a rich, muddy brown. The scene was completely filled with serpents mostly of the same color, with patterns inscribed upon their bodies.

Sometimes the serpents were white with rainbow patterns running along the length of their bodies. I could feel these serpents enter my body and fill it with energy. They seemed to be the agents of the re-patterning of my body. And when I saw them coming toward me, I was overwhelmed with an indescribable joy.

What I have concluded is that the ayahuasca approaches the body with a kind of *tough love*. The force of its approach is often so strong that the natural reaction of the body and personality is to defend against it, keep it out, meet it with fear, and push it away. What often results is a kind of battle narrated by a mind that may project hostility. Some minds project a sense of evil upon this aggressive intruder, and the fearful mind may construct imagery that gives substance to such a projection.

For myself, that battle did not occur in any seriously challenging way apart from a fear of dying in my very first ceremony. But I have witnessed huge battles waged by some of my companions over the course of many ceremonies. I have similarly witnessed most of them coming to the other shore, transcending what seemed from an outside perspective a perfect storm of internally experienced challenges. Most expressed some ultimate experience of love, even if it took several ceremonies to get to that point. For many, that love seemed heaven-sent, judging from their descriptions of traveling away from the earth into the cosmos, encounters with Christ or angelic beings, or some other return to heaven.

I don't recall hearing from someone else the powerful experience of love that occurred for me while being taken deep into the heart of the earth. However, there seems to be a transformative experience of love waiting at some point and in some way on the other side of this rigorous crossing.

Observing that, it occurred to me that a sensible preparation for the experience might be to help people learn to open themselves to the medicine in a non-defensive way. My work began to center on the role of attention, and how to hold it in our own hearts as a means of creating the sense of love and safety in the body that would more readily welcome the bitter medicine and challenging experiences.

As I began to teach this process to my companions, I received feedback that it helped them to move through the ceremonies with less fear, a greater sense of love and safety, and more receptivity to the experience that was to come. The process of meeting the plant became less combative and more collaborative. I sensed a collaboration between the soul and the medicine, both approaching the damaged areas of the body with love and the assurance that all is well or will turn out that way.

Beginning to work more intensively with the huachuma began to give me a better perspective on the process of the ayahuasca. In my experience, the huachuma took an altogether different approach and served a somewhat different purpose, yet one that suggested a possible collaboration between these two powerful plants.

Huachuma

The histories written about huachuma always include the stories of the Spanish priest who named the plant San Pedro. He called the plant Saint Peter because he believed it opened the gates of heaven.

Like ayahuasca, huachuma was traditionally used at night. In Peru's spiritual tourism milieu, however, huachuma has come to be a plant used more often during the day. My first experiences were in 2004 and occurred at night, facilitated by a longtime huachumero in the Sacred Valley of southern Peru where the engagement between the spiritual tourists and the huachuma is common.

The shaman dispensed doses that were small and bitter, reminding me of the taste of ayahuasca. As various people have described their experience of the plant to me, they often speak of its softness, saying that it brought them to the experience of connection and sometimes to an experience of ecstasy.

For me, those initial experiences were indeed mild, giving rise to a certain feeling of sensuality that did not rise to what I regard as ecstasy such as I have encountered, even early on, with the ayahuasca. On one or more occasions with the huachuma, I experienced nausea, which seemed to surprise the shaman.

These particular ceremonies lasted for three or four hours. During these, the shaman rattled, sang *icaros*, and attended to one participant or another. Icaros are the songs traditionally sung by shamans during an ayahuasca ceremony. I have not heard them sung by any other huachumero since. Years later, I concluded that this shaman's approach to the work was to give a relatively small dose, sufficient to open the body to a process of healing that he facilitated, but not so large as to take the body into a deeper experience that might have other effects.

When I had occasion to work with this same shaman again, I had a particularly difficult experience that involved abdominal pain and some nausea, neither of which I had prior to the ceremony. He told me after the ceremony that I was being used by the medicine as a surrogate. He described watching the energy body of one of the other participants cross the room and enter my body so that it would be available to him to do his work for the other person. The other person, he said, was resisting the medicine, which found another way to get the work done by using my body. I did not bring this up with the other person, feeling it inappropriate to do so, and I had no validation of the shaman's interpretation of these events.

Sometime later, I had a one-on-one ceremony with a female apprentice of the same shaman. Again, the ceremony occurred at night. The shamana gave me a more dilute but much larger dose that I immediately purged with great force. She promptly offered me another dose of the same size. For the next eight hours, my body shook as though my neurological system had been plugged into an electrical socket. The small love seat I was leaning against as I sat on the floor of her living room beat a steady drum-like rhythm on the wall for most of that time.

During that ceremony, I experienced being dragged through the universe by the Hindu goddess Kali, the physical symptoms of giving birth, and the ability to translate a language completely unfamiliar to me that was channeled by the shamana. There was nothing sensual or ecstatic about the experience, and the meaning that I eventually attached to my experience would not come forward until years later when I had another occasion to drink the medicine.

It was seven years later when I returned to Peru in 2011 that I began to re-engage the huachuma. All of my experiences from this point forward occurred during the day. These more recent experiences included medicine freshly cooked from the cactus as well as powdered forms of the plant dispensed in some water or fruit juice to wash it down.

These more recent experiences also seemed only little related to the popular notions of soft connectivity that surrounded this medicine. When I have taken the full dose, my experience has been deeply intense and difficult to navigate. The medicine is strongly present in the body for a longer time than with ayahuasca. In some ways, it feels more rigorous than my experiences with the ayahuasca. Nausea is often but not always a part of my physical response to the huachuma.

With the full dose, I have visions. The visions are different in nature to those I've experienced with the ayahuasca. My ayahuasca visions are more three-dimensional, full screen, with the eye held steady for longer scenes. The huachuma has offered quicker, dimmer, yet profoundly compelling clips that are sometimes archetypal, sometimes symbolic, and sometimes literal.

On the other hand, there is a parallel in terms of information. With both plants, I often receive information directly, as though channeled, along with visuals that are themselves informational.

I have never experienced a former life with ayahuasca, and I have for many years treated the significance of former lives with skepticism. My experience and reading incline me to believe that our souls carry an energetic imprint from the lives the soul has experienced in the past. However, it has been my impression that many people get attached to stories of former lives, accurate or not, that complicate the ego story with which they are already grappling. I had felt that my current life contained all the information I needed to enable me to resolve the issues that needed to be resolved. The huachuma brought me to another view.

With the huachuma, the engagement with former lives has been a common experience and has provided a meaningful and helpful source of information about the life I am now living. I have had several experiences in which it felt as though I was able to look through the eyes of a human who lived in a former time and could thereby see what was happening at that time.

I cannot say whether or not I was experiencing my former life, but what I was able to observe suggested a history of experience that I carry in my body now. It has given me a longer, deeper view of the human enterprise, and more compassion for both the difficulty and grinding slowness, at least in human terms, of its progress.

I could see a thread of identity connecting various former lives to this one, but what I saw was not ego-fulfillment material. Often to the contrary, my experiences of former lives included being in positions of power in which I—or the person through whose I eyes I was looking—abused and manipulated others. Part of what I witnessed was a struggle to transcend those propensities as well.

My experiences of former lives with the huachuma suggest to me that the plant works to a greater degree with the soul than the body, since it is the soul that may carry the imprints of former lives, even if that imprint is imparted to the body of this turn on the planet. Even though my experience with former lives has been limited to the huachuma, I have heard stories of ayahuasca experiences that involve former lives, which certainly are relevant to the patterns held by the body that are addressed by the ayahuasca.

With time, I have found that taking a quarter of what is regarded as a full dose of huachuma allows me to have a soft and connective experience, while a full dose takes me into a realm of archetypes and an interactive engagement with them. As my body seemed to sensitize to the huachuma, even a small dose could have the latter effect.

The general field of engagement seems to be cosmic, in the direction of heaven, rather than downward into the belly of matter and the earth fields I have experienced with ayahuasca. In this more rigorous engagement, I do not have the deep experience of love and safety that the ayahuasca has afforded me, but neither do I feel afraid.

With a larger dose, my body occasionally has the experience of being taken over by one of a few archetypal figures that present themselves. Sometimes I share my body with the archetypal figure, giving me the opportunity to experience the particular quality and extraordinary strength of the archetypal field. Sometimes, my presence is pushed aside such that I feel myself to be an observer. In other words, sometimes I sense that I am in the body, and sometimes not.

My being out of body may be occasioned by the action of some field of intelligence that is motivated to take the body as its own for the moment. This very possibility requires a skillful engagement with the medicine, one that includes a means of protection against predatory energies that would take advantage of this openness in the body to enter the body as well. This is why it is important not to use these medicines without the skill to create that protection or the help of someone else who can do it for you. For me, that skill involves a deep grounding in the body through the field of the heart. This is a skill that is developed, like most skills, over time with disciplined practice.

These archetypal experiences seem to present an opportunity for understanding the nature of our connection to the universe. One of my persistent experiences with ayahuasca is that the creative power of the earth is represented by the archetypal dragon and serpent. I consistently see serpents in a variety of shapes, sizes, and color combinations. When I experience these serpents, my entire being is filled with joy. Sometimes I see them outside of myself, most often moving toward me. When I experience these serpents entering me, I see them as the animating force of the matter that enacts the design programs of my own body, continually moving, restoring, and building. The archetypal dragon seems to be the totality of the energy that is expressed more minutely in the form of the individual small serpents. Sometimes the dragon is seen as the cosmic boa often represented in shamanic art.

As the huachuma ceremonies took a more dramatic turn in 2011, I experienced the added element of the jaguar archetype. That field of intelligence had appeared in my very first ceremony with ayahuasca in 2000, when I felt the jaguar enter my body and provide the physical strength necessary to push through an experience of purging that I thought might end in my death.

In my first 2011 huachuma ceremony, I felt the jaguar enter again and empower my body to participate in a dance in which I felt the dragon archetype energy beneath my feet and the Kali archetype above me. I felt as though the archetypes were dancing through me. The shaman facilitating this ceremony sat briefly with me as the neurological effects were giving rise to some anxiety on my part that my body was being damaged. He made a tea from the purple flowers of the tree located just outside the maloka. Then he handed me a drum, which helped me to self-regulate and be present to the force of this extraordinary energy over the next several hours.

Ceremonies in 2012 have brought new and more powerful archetypal experiences, along with a new respect for the power of this medicine. Some who speak of huachuma seem to minimize its power and effect compared to ayahuasca. Because of that sense, the huachuma is often treated with less respect, and used with minimal or no ceremony. There are, however, accounts of miraculous healings occurring with both medicines. My own experience forces me to a conclusion that both of these medicines are powerful in different ways, and that each leads to healing and transformation.

With the new perspective offered by Don Umberto's point that pacos are not shamans but mystics, another view of the huachuma arises. If huachuma opens the gates to heaven, it is a tool that reaches toward the upper realms that are the domain of mysticism even as it is a tool employed by shamans. It is a plant that engages the soul more, perhaps, than the body even as its means is to approach the body softly. Its work perhaps parallels the object of Q'ero mysticism, but from a shamanic approach that is open to the use of plants to create the experience of connectivity. In my opinion, it could be said to occupy a stance between the two. It is a practice of the middle. So it is not surprising to learn that it grows well above the lower world of the jungle, but below the upper world of the mountains. It grows best, I'm told, in the higher altitude near Huaraz, Peru, around 10,000 feet (3,050 meters).

Thoughts of Collaboration

One of the ayahuasca centers where Darlene and I worked had a schedule of four ayahuasca ceremonies in eight days, followed by a huachuma day without ceremony. The theory—and so much of this is theory—was that the experience of the huachuma would provide a day of rest from the rigor of the ayahuasca by providing an opportunity for gentle communion with the flowers and trees. In this way, the theory went, the rigorous effects of the ayahuasca on the body could be softened and perhaps better integrated. And for some people, that seemed to be the case.

When I experienced these plants in close proximity, the experience of the huachuma was more rigorous than the ayahuasca. Contrary to the expectations of the center's facilitator, who dispensed the huachuma without ceremony, it exhausted my body. The huachuma kept me in its embrace perhaps twice as long as the ayahuasca and did not leave me feeling stronger. Its effects were both dramatic and confusing.

My experiences seemed significantly different than those of my companions, who reported more of the soft and connective feelings that were anticipated. Without the guidance of a good huachumero who could place this experience into some kind of cognitive context for me, I was reluctant to go further in my experimentation with the huachuma. But the experiences were so compelling that I was reluctant not to.

As I have inquired about huachumeros, I have been told by an ayahuasquero for whom I have considerable respect that he has not met a master huachumero. Sometimes, he says, the plants and the fields of intelligence that use them are the only teachers of resort and we have to learn directly from the plants themselves. This is how the process probably started between humans and the plants. The same ayahuasquero has said that his master teachers say they continue to learn from the plants, ceremony by ceremony.

So many questions remain. New questions are now being raised by the advent of a spiritual tourism in which postmodern consciousness is showing up for ceremony in Peru for the first time after thousands of years of indigenous use. Westerners are coming to the plants for a different purpose than the way the plants have been traditionally used by shamans for physical healing and restoration of the soul of a troubled villager. The plants are now working with a new audience, and the dynamic is changing as consciousness itself is working in a different context.

Taking all of those observations into account, I reached a few working hypotheses.

I see that a critical initial step in the healing of the body and encouragement of soul emergence is to help the body feel safe and loved. Two simple strategies can be used to accomplish this. First, the participant can learn to differentiate the soul from the body. This allows the soul to position itself in relation to the field of the heart in such a way that, in conjunction with an appropriate breathing technique, a sense of love and safety can be cultivated in the body before the medicine is taken. Second, by using smaller doses of the huachuma that are titrated with experience to an individual's own need and capacity, it is likely that the participant's body will be more willing to open to the medicine. Smaller initial doses of ayahuasca could have the same effect.

This approach might more often elicit the sense of love and safety that would allow the medicine to do the necessary work without the conflict that frequently comes from an unconsciously held fear that resists the medicine even when the participant has purposely chosen to take it.

I also sense that a central objective of the soul's work is to create a partnership between the soul and body that serves the soul's destiny. This partnership is the objective of what we could call the soul's embodiment and is often referred to as "grounding."

Remembering the priest's perspective that huachuma opens the gates of heaven, I would agree. The huachuma facilitates grounding by reminding the soul who it is, reminding the soul of its home in heaven, and reminding the soul that it can be the agent of love for the body. In this way, the newly awakened soul has a greater capacity to bring the love of heaven to the body. In this way, the body may have an experience of love and safety in the arms of heaven without the necessity of finding its way to the sense of love and safety in the earth that comes through a deep experience with the ayahuasca.

From this perspective, the orientation of the huachuma is upward. My sense is that it talks more with the soul, and perhaps does something in the nature of helping winnow the soul out of its slumbering enmeshment in the body so that the soul can come to the self-awareness that it *is* a soul.

The huachuma reminds the soul who it is, where it came from, how prior incarnations can inform its present work, and what its work is. The huachuma can, in this way, give the body a taste of heaven's love without deeply invading the body in the way of the ayahuasca. Huachuma heightens the senses and allows us to experience the body's physical environment as non-threatening at the same time as it draws our attention out rather than in. Although the experiences of these medicines are inherently internal, the huachuma experience of the soul touches more into the external nature of the soul relative to the body.

The ayahuasca, conversely, goes immediately toward the body. If the body resists enough, the ayahuasca may take the consciousness away from the body and into the cosmos. If it does take the consciousness out in this way, the soul may have the same experience of coming into self-awareness that the huachuma facilitates, and there may be a similar experience of connection that we may feel as heaven's love. With the ayahuasca, this preliminary sense of connection with heaven may in turn facilitate the sense of love and safety for the body that permits the medicine a greater possibility of pushing past the body's defensive reaction.

On the other hand, the ayahuasca may simply push itself into the body, confronting the defenses of the body directly, in which case its presence may feel invasive.

However the ayahuasca gains access to the body, it can cleanse the defensive patterns by which the body holds the soul and heaven at bay. With those defenses pushed aside, the ayahuasca can take us deeper into the realm of the earth's heart and its love. From this perspective, the trajectory of the ayahuasca is downward. The focus of the ayahuasca is on the body rather than the soul, unless it needs to awaken the soul to enlist the soul's help with the body. The ayahuasca's ultimate function, to infer from my own experience, is to heal the body of its patterns of fear and remind the body of who it is and where it came from. When the body experiences the earth energies that represent its origin, it also experiences the extraordinary power associated with its earth origin.

Ayahuasca seems to mesmerize and capture the attention, bringing it more and more into the body, even if it is taken out of the body first as the body gradually yields in the light of a heavenly experience. While the softness of huachuma might bring us into the body in an initial experience, it may be doing so to wrest the soul's attention from its enmeshment with the body so that heaven may speak to the soul.

With its comforting way, huachuma seems to anesthetize the body, so that its defenses are not triggered in such a way that they would otherwise monopolize the attention of the immature soul, allowing the soul a brief return to the sense of heaven's love. There the soul encounters fields of information that remind it who it is.

In other words, the ayahuasca may ultimately work more deeply in the body, while huachuma may work at the level of heaven's connection, more in the shallows of the body. While we may be apt to go out of body with ayahuasca's first blast, the ultimate effect of the ayahuasca is to provide just the opposite experience.

When we see these two medicines from this perspective of viewing the soul distinct from a body in which it has become enmeshed, we can see the combination of the two medicines potentially providing a more complete coverage of the issues with which humans struggle. One plant addresses the soul more directly, the other the body.

For one individual, the softer entry with the huachuma might be indicated. For another, the ayahuasca might be the better choice. There seems little harm in experimenting to see what works, so long as the process is engaged in the context of competently facilitated ceremony with appropriate preparation, respectful intention, focused engagement, and attentive integration.

Having made these distinctions between the actions of the ayahuasca and the huachuma, it remains important to remember that behind the plants are ineffable intelligences that provide healing to soul and body in a way that is unique to each person who engages them. Specific outcomes are unpredictable. Both plants are equally powerful in distinct ways. In any situation, either plant may be able to accomplish the healing necessary for the day, and we need to follow our hearts and intuition in coming to our meetings with the respective plants.

I sense that these plants are presenting themselves to assist the evolution of human consciousness in a very large way, as is evidenced by the huge number of searching souls who feel literally "called" to work with them. I say "plants are presenting themselves" quite intentionally, since my own experience compels me to look no longer at the presence or the effects of the plants as coincidental, or to view the plants as devoid of intelligence. The benefit that the plants provide to the process of soul evolution is too powerful and precise to be coincidental, and the scent of intentional design around the relationship between plants and humans too strong.

Bringing these plants into a postmodern milieu for the benefit of a new audience will take some fresh thinking grounded in deeper knowings. Soul tribes that come together around a tambo that chooses to work with these medicines can serve the purpose of developing the processes and environments that can best provide effective preparation, support, and integration of the plant experience. The ultimate purpose of that community is to support soul emergence with a variety of tools and strategies of which plants are only a part.

10

SOUL TRIBES AND TAMBOS

A Support Community with a Soul Perspective

WHEN WE ADOPT A SOUL PERSPECTIVE, the purpose of the human enterprise comes more clearly into view. I have a soul perspective when I can say from a position of direct and self-aware internal experience that

⊚ *I am a soul*

⊚ *I am on the planet to learn those lessons that will allow me to transcend my fate and create my destiny*

⊚ *My destiny requires me to fully engage and explore the dimension of earth and the density of matter to the degree and in the manner dictated by my own unique and very individual soul nature*

⊚ *My ultimate purpose is to serve the process that is the substance of the evolution of consciousness and the open-ended creation of the universe, and*

⊚ *For all of this to happen, I must learn to become a messenger who communicates heaven's design into earth's matrix of matter and become an active and skilled connector between the two.*

To get traction on this challenging list, awakening souls need a community of soul support, whether their ultimate work of destiny is within or without the mainstream communities through which the patriarchy continues to maintain control. Soul support is the central and defining function that evolving soul communities must provide. That support can come in many ways.

So with these thoughts in mind, how might we envision the tambo by which a soul tribe seeks to create the infrastructure for such support? And what would be the necessary elements?

The Prime Process Objective

The three most important questions faced by humans have never changed: Who am I? What is my purpose? And how do I answer the first two questions?

Certainly, views on the answers to these questions will differ. Some might point out that questions that pertain to survival are primary. I would agree that survival is foundational. But survival to what end?

These three questions not only give fundamental meaning to survival, but drive the underlying impulse that makes us fight to survive. Just a little introspection helps us to discover that we are here for a purpose. Death does not defeat that purpose, but provides just one more opportunity to define it. The meaning I bring to the process of my dying is far more important than the fact of my dying.

My views on how to answer these three questions are deeply colored by the experiences of my own life, and by what I have heard whispered by the ancestors in ancient temples that still function as portals for the voices of those earlier earth travelers and other fields of intelligence that wish to connect with us.

My sense is that the common work of a certain group of souls here on the planet—what I'll call the *prime process objective*—is what I mentioned in the first part of this book, which is to receive, embody, protect, evolve, record, and translate the processes by which human souls co-evolve with the planetary soul in service of the creation of the universe.

The work of these souls is to dialogue with the myriad fields of intelligence that inhabit what we often call heaven, cosmos, and earth. The work is to bridge this dimension to other-dimensional fields of intelligence that seek to support the evolution of human consciousness in service of the evolution of consciousness itself. The group's work is to understand, explore, and embody heaven's engagement with matter. And its work is to pass on the knowledge. Of course, all humans are in some way involved with this same work, because all of us are inherently involved in the evolution of consciousness whether we are conscious of it or not.

There is a particular aspect of this work that is understood by all souls that are in a process of awakening to who they are. These souls know that the longstanding patriarchal hegemony has dishonored, disregarded, and decimated the feminine in all its planetary forms. They know that all of us are responsible to reach out to the feminine and raise it to its full power and dignity.

What is perhaps less understood is that the process of raising the feminine up inherently demands that the masculine also rise to its full power and dignity. That power and dignity is obviously not expressed by the patriarchy even if the emergence of the unconscious masculine into this patriarchal form represented the necessary evolutionary step of the masculine emerging out of the feminine. Just as children must create an identity separate from that of the mother, the human masculine of any gender has had to emerge from an unconscious relationship with the earth Mother that characterized early human consciousness. The masculine has now emerged over an evolutionary time period into the equivalent of a teenager in a full hormone-driven rebellion, still too immature to drive the family car. Unfortunately, the patriarchal adolescent has run off with the keys, and it's quickly approaching midnight.

The raising of the feminine is not for the purpose of transplanting the masculine with the feminine, even though the patriarchy must fall in that process. Neither feminine nor masculine is superior to the other. It is not a matter of replacing a patriarchy with a matriarchy. Rather, we must discover in the masculine and feminine both their inherent complementarity and their equal dignity and power in the midst of their inherent differences. We must discover the synergies between them, along with the potentials for their collaboration. And both need to be called to their maturity in the same breath.

During my recent time with the Q'ero, I heard another perspective on this process. The concepts of masculine and feminine, I understood Don Umberto to say, do not describe the totality of the duality in which we live. Rather, there is duality in general: masculine/feminine, yin/yang, male/female, inner/outer, up/down, left/right, and so on. The Q'ero describe this more general polarity as *yanintin*. Yanintin represents two connected but different qualities that have the potential to operate in complementary fashion. When they do so, they form a relationship, a third thing distinct from the two separate things. That third thing is the manifestation of the potential of the two, and it is called *masintin*.

Soul and body, for example, are inherently connected, but remain in unconscious and unpotentiated relationship until the soul awakens and leads the body into a conscious partnership. Until that happens, the soul and body form a polarity that remains only in a potential state. The potential is a yanintin. When the two can form a balanced relationship and evoke the higher potential of collaboration, they form a masintin. The process of creation requires that we move from the potential of polarity (connection) into the materialization of collaboration (relationship). Moving from yanintin to masintin at all levels possible for humans is our work.

And, importantly, there is urgency to the work. The Western hegemony of neoliberal capitalistic globalism is moving with great momentum toward a disastrous end. So the work of at least one large group of awakening souls is to gather the process knowledge that the ancestors have accumulated and to evolve it. We *are* the ancestors fast forwarded into a present to which our own choices have fated and destined us to return. The process knowledge is the understanding and conscious embodiment of the yanintin and how it forms the masintin.

We are here to pick up this process where we left it off before, but now in different circumstances with different challenges. We need to take stock, take a breath, and begin again. And we need to find a way to protect what has been learned from the disaster that the immature masculine force of globalization represents as we move the process knowledge one step further.

This is the prime process objective.

The considerations that follow address possible means of accomplishing this objective.

Elders

I see a *core team of elders* who come together to create a prototype from among several possibilities for a tambo community. "Elder," like "old soul," is not an age category, but a person with a skill set that contributes to the accomplishment of the prime process objective.

These elders are responsible for creating the agreement that defines the purpose of the community and for selecting the place where the tribe will gather. They might number as few as one or two, but could number many more. The fewer, however, the easier it is to reach the initial agreement from which the tambo proceeds. But with more, the greater the range of skills and talents the elders can offer to those who look to the tambo and tribe for support.

The skill sets required of the elders are ultimately as broad as the list of necessaries that a sustainable community created for the support of souls requires. That list can be inferred from the discussion below.

The Agreement

For a coherent community to arise, the founding elders must have a shared vision and mission that are fueled with passion and incorporated into a flexible and evolving curriculum. Those elements need to be incorporated into an agreement upon how the tambo will operate.

The purpose of the agreement is to define the overall process by which a tambo can serve the prime process objective. Because no particular vision is sufficient for an indefinite time, tribes need to hold themselves in the space of vision continuously and revise the agreement accordingly. The vision space is the heart.

When the heart can perceive a vision that provides direction for a time, the mind can help with planning the actions that define the mission that implements the new vision. The mission of a particular time will evolve again when the heart receives a new vision. This continual attention to the heart field as a source of vision keeps passion at the forefront of the tambo's work and relevancy to the guiding agreement.

A Curriculum

The Soul's Critical Path created a conceptual lens that might guide the creation of a curriculum. It suggested several discrete stages of soul evolution that can help us to understand the process of soul maturation in which all of us are engaged, as well as the kind of support that is necessary at each stage.

These conceptual stages can help to define the point at which particular interventions may assist a soul to move forward in its own evolution. Tambos can be of immediate benefit to those souls leaning out of Stage Two. Souls in Stage Two remain asleep in the body, invited by pain or discomfort to awaken to the memory that they are souls on the planet for a purpose. These souls need help in experiencing themselves as souls, and they need help in learning how to control attention.

Souls who have reached Stage Three already experience themselves as souls and need a different kind of facilitation. They need help to remove from the body those dysfunctional patterns that arose from early wounding, and they need help in learning to focus attention both in the heart and soul. When these steps are taken from an experiential soul perspective rather than the predominantly secular psychological approach that gives primacy to personality while it neglects the very existence of the soul, then this work can move forward much more quickly. Nevertheless, psychology has contributed to our understandings of the very patterns of personality that we seek to address. Consequently, it is important to honor the successes and failures of psychology for what those lessons contribute to this stage of soul learning, which is concerned with transforming the personality into a viable vehicle for the soul.

As old patterns are resolved and attention skills are developed during Stages Three and Four, these evolving souls may remain with or visit the tambo again for a time to deepen their work of Stage Five. That exploration begins when the more mature soul turns its attention toward its relationship with matter and the opportunities for the creative work of destiny. Each soul stands in yanintin potential with the dimension of matter that we know as the earth realm.

The job of Stage Five souls is to move beyond that potential to the level of manifestation that represents masintin and the work of creation itself. It is at this stage that the soul explores more deeply the various dimensions of both heaven and earth and the intelligent fields that attend the soul's process. Those souls will move on to do that deeper work in various places in the world to which they are called.

Across all three stages of soul evolution, the curriculum would reinforce two primary elements. The first would be a process of helping people to learn how to *connect.* This stage involves learning how to infuse the personality with a clear soul identity; learning to develop the soul skills of attention that are necessary for the soul to anchor itself in the portal of the heart field; learning how to use the portal of the heart to connect the soul to body, heaven, and earth; and developing an understanding of how a soul overcomes fate and begins to create its destiny. This first part brings a soul to the understanding and experience of the yanintin.

The second aspect of a soul curriculum would build on the ability to use that inherent connection by teaching the skills of *relationship*. The awareness of our inherent connection with everything, and our ability to experience that connection, are not the same as the ability to function in relationship, whether it be a relationship between soul and body, or with other humans, plants, or the fields of intelligence that surround us. Before we can competently relate, we must learn how to experience connection. Then we can use connection as the foundation for building relationship. This second part brings a soul to the understanding and experience of masintin.

In these ways, the tambo can serve souls at all stages of soul evolution. Facilitating a flow of awakening souls through the tambos will serve the prime process objective that is critical to the continuing expansion and evolution of consciousness.

As souls move on, they will leave with an invitation to return to the tambos, which will remain available to provide those working souls with the respite and retuning we all require. The tambo and tribe can provide a welcoming home, support for the next step of learning, and blessings upon the soul's departure, with the invitation to return with welcome once again. With all of these supportive elements in place, a soul might find its way to its own work of destiny in a shorter time frame than the soul working alone could accomplish.

Place

Although the prime process objective can be supported anywhere at any time, there are settings with optimal qualities. These qualities come in two forms, both of which may be either natural or cultivated.

The first is an environment that holds, supports, and nurtures the human body and thereby makes the process of the soul's cultivation of the body's cooperation easier. Temperate climate, an absence of pollution and noise, an abundance of plants and trees, a reliable source of clean water, land capable of growing food sufficient for the needs of the small community, and so on—we all have a picture of such a place in our minds—are essential.

Such a place is the physical analog of the Garden of Eden, a concentration of the generative qualities of nature. It is not the harsh and isolated environment sometimes chosen for the purpose of hardening the spirit. The world and fate provide enough of that without our creating more, and enough of that may well be imposed by the impending failure of the present forces of global commercialization. Consequently, the tambo is probably best located away from the distractions and chaos of Stage Two culture, as far as possible. Yet the tambo must be integrated into communities to which it is adjacent and upon which it is ultimately dependent. So there is a balance of which we have heard before. The tambo must be in the world, and also of it, even as it provides a nurturing home and a teaching function.

The second quality of place is more subtle, one that most of us cannot see but can learn to sense. There are many places in the world that function as portals or vortices. A portal is something like a standing wave of frequencies that constitute a doorway through which communication with other-dimensional fields of intelligence can more easily occur.

We have called such places sacred. I don't prefer to divide the world into the sacred and non-sacred, since there is nothing that is, for me, not a part of the whole to which I give the name God. I see these places merely as more conducive to communication. These places that amplify our connection with other dimensions help us to do our work in the same way that the entheogenic plants do, by collaborating with our own skills of connection, relationship, and communication.

If such a place can be found and a tambo located nearby, all the better. If not, then such a place needs to be cultivated. I say nearby, because the intensity of the energy that facilitates communication is not always conducive to day-to-day living. Its power can create a feeling of imbalance and chaos. Indeed, part of the skill set of a maturing soul is to be able to maintain focus of attention despite the intensity of such energies. More information is coming into our dense world right now, and we need to learn both to hear it and live in relationship with the energetic fields that facilitate it.

Right Relationship with Place

While we might look at place in terms of whether the geography is hospitable and energies supportive, the creation of *right relationship* between tribe and place is yet a further process. The Q'ero call this right relationship *ayni*.

Ayni implies the assumption of responsibility for the human role in supporting the viability of the earth as the foundation of our request that earth support the viability of the tribe. Ayni translates well into the notion of reciprocity. Reciprocity means that yanintin (potential of manifestation) can move into masintin (manifestation of potential) when there is balance in the energy of exchange between the two parts of the polarity.

Our own soul work requires each of us to become a powerful connection between heaven and the density of matter. Soul tribes have the same responsibility. Even if we find a place that provides an enhanced opportunity for communication, what I mean to emphasize here is the obligation to *use* that connection, and to use it with an attitude of gratitude, honor, and respect for the obligation of reciprocity.

Right relationship requires our transcending connection (yanintin) into relationship (masintin) and doing so with an assumption of responsibility appropriate to the highest level of soul maturity we can muster. The relationship with place must be cultivated with the same loving attention we devote to cultivating personal relationships.

Sustainability requires a relationship of reciprocity. Heaven connects with earth through a soul and a body. Earth connects with heaven through a body and a soul. Each and all are responsible to the others for a relationship of sustainability. This is *ayni*.

So, a central function of the soul tribe is to perform, model, and teach the skill of sustaining ayni with earth and heaven in general, with the place of the tambo in particular, between body and soul, and with each other.

Ceremony and Prayer

In 2013, Darlene and I visited an Inca site that had not been restored or protected by the government. Our expedition of an afternoon was led by Filia, a Peruvian woman who speaks five languages including her native Quechua.

The site is not widely known outside of the local area, but had recently been the subject of an article in a regional newspaper. Filia was anxious to visit this site and do ceremony there because the article included an announcement that the government would be closing the site soon to begin protection and restoration work. The closure would preclude our doing ceremony there.

When we met Filia and her husband Dieter to start the short drive from our home to the site, Filia had a bag full of items for the ceremony. Darlene and I had the same in our backpacks. Pepe, another friend of Filia, arrived with his pack full of photographic equipment.

We found the site located two or three hundred meters up a steep slope and beneath stark rock outcrops in a narrow river valley, just above the track for the trains that run daily between Cusco and Machu Picchu. The unique physical aspect of the site is a black monolith that bears three *chacanas*—sometimes called the Incan or Andean cross—carved with the beautiful symmetry and precision that is characteristic of the Incan culture. This stone had suffered significant damage from looters who had dynamited it in hopes of finding treasure beneath.

While Pepe recorded with his cameras, the rest of us laid out items from our own altars, along with incense, flowers, and candles. We said our prayers and spent some quiet time before heading back down the hill.

Days later, Pepe asked me what it was that we did, since it was not apparent to him even as he filmed our activities and listened to the out-loud portion of our prayers. What I explained to him described the role that ceremony plays as a foundation for the engagement with the place in which the tambo is located.

When we approach an ancient site like this, we do so with inherent respect for the ancestors who have preceded us. We don't need to know much about them in order to start a conversation. We know that, however they conceived their work, they were connecting with guidance from other dimensions. Connecting and interacting with this same guidance is a large part of our work, so we appreciate the work of those who have laid out a path before us, including the energy they have invested in creating or cultivating a place where such communication is supported.

We assume that the symbols that may have been invested in a particular site, such as the chacanas we found in this site, may reflect a multiplicity of understandings of human relationship to the universe and all its dimensions. We impose no judgments upon the particular understandings that may have attended use of the site since we assume that the site has been created over time by people whose work was consistent with the prime process objective as they saw it.

When we enter such a site, consequently, we are feeling for the presence of other-dimensional beings and for the kind of energies that indicate the presence of a portal. These beings might include the spirits of the very ancestors who created and protected the site during their lifetimes and who chose to remain and devote their soul energies to its continuing power and protection.

We first acknowledge and honor those ancestors and their work. Then we ask their permission to use this site and be present in it. We ask them to be present for the work we propose as a continuation of their work. In this way, we see ourselves as part of an unbroken chain of humans who have done this work throughout human history. In some sites, I have heard the ancestral voices speak their request and their hope that we who are present will not break the ancestral chain of those who have done this work before us.

With these preliminaries completed, our attention turns to the ultimate purpose of the ceremony. We have come to use the portal, if there is one present, in order to amplify our connection to the other-dimensional fields of intelligence that attend the human enterprise. We may know these fields by several archetypal names and qualities that are recognized in one way or another by all indigenous peoples, or we may not. We ask for their attention and thank them for their presence. And then we listen. If there is connection, we sometimes respond in dialogue. Sometimes we have questions, and other times not. It is a process to which we return time and again.

Some people call this process *prayer*, and I often use that word for that purpose. But there is a qualification to my use of that word which feels important to me regarding the very nature of souls and soul work.

If I get on my knees, it is a way of paying respect and also reminding myself of the deep level of attention that needs to be paid in a particular moment. It is not an indication that my soul is less important or inferior in any way to the infinite intelligence of which my soul is an inherent part and critically important agent.

Getting on my knees is rather an indication of my intention to attend this ceremonial function with a deep humility that acknowledges the mystery of the universe as far greater than my physically embedded soul/mind can hope to understand, and that humility is a necessary condition of the state of curiosity which our human process of creating demands. Other-dimensional beings are important players in the divine plan, but they function more as partners for souls, and souls are themselves just as important in the grand scheme.

Souls find themselves on the front line of consciousness evolution, doing the dirty work of engaging matter. I have, on occasion, found myself challenging those fields of intelligence to be a bit more humble in their injunctions to me, reminding them that, if they think this is so easy, they can come down and, by God, do it themselves. NASA, I'm sure, operates with the same humility when requesting their astronauts to perform a task that can't be accomplished by pushing buttons at mission control. If angels could do the whole work of creation with buttons, souls would not be necessary.

So prayer is a reciprocal process, a two-way street, and is the basis for communicating about a project that is just too important for humor and humility to be absent from either side. I don't often get a sense that angels have a sense of humor, but there have been hints that they are learning.

A key aspect of the ceremony is the remembrance that this work is optimally done through the heart, which is itself a portal—the one which gives human consciousness its most powerful access to those other dimensions. Consequently, prayer practice involves the remembrance of the importance of practicing the skill of holding attention in the heart.

From this perspective, ceremony is a fundamental aspect of the relationship with the place of the tambo and our creation of right relationship all around.

However it is done, and whatever its purpose on a particular day, ceremony is about communication and an exchange of information. That exchange may come in the form of a download of a healing vibration or program analogous to the updating of the operating system of your computer. Or it may simply be a conversation, an opportunity to check in, to kick an idea around, or to find a different way of conceptualizing the challenge we face in the moment.

The tambo and tribe cannot perform their ultimate function without skillful attention paid to this kind of communication, whether one prefers to call it ceremony or not. The plant medicine engagement is an optional subcategory of this larger ceremonial imperative, one that has the potential to enlarge our capacity to interact with those who are out there ready to help us do the work here.

Awe-Ful Science

Tambos will not function without science.
There is the science of the mind. And there is the science of the heart-mind.

When science looks solely through the lens of the mind, it separates and analyzes. It breaks a thing down into its smallest parts in the hope of understanding its essence. While there is value in understanding the parts and their relationship to each other, this science sometimes fails to understand that the essence of life cannot be discovered in the parts.

In the process of analysis, science often treats the entire world—the earth, plants, animals, and humans—as parts. Our human experience of this treatment is to feel a-part, isolated, vulnerable, and separated from everything else. As a consequence, the mind's perspective, acting alone, inevitably engenders fear in the body.

It is an *awful* science that operates from the mind alone. Yet the potential of the mind is evident in the extraordinary accomplishments of even this kind of science.

Not all science is awful. Operating within this science that breaks things down is a science that is grounded in the heart. When we look at the world through the lens of the heart, we do not break things down. Rather, our souls peer through the heart as a lens that uses connection as a way of gathering information about the object of our curiosity.

With our hearts, we feel into and experience things in their wholeness. When we see the wholeness of a thing as its essence, we are able also to see the parts in a way that gives rise to an understanding beyond what the mind operating alone can accomplish.

We know the way of looking through the heart as a sense of appreciation, of *awe,* just as we would stand transfixed before the beauty of a sunset. If we can hold onto the awe as we transform our gaze stereoscopically to include the view of the mind, we have a far better chance of seeing the wholeness of a thing while achieving some understanding of its parts in a process of vibrant and dynamic operation. We might be able to watch how a thing works without separating it from the very mystery of creation of which it is an integral part. This is *awe-ful* science.

My friend Jerry, an American living in Peru, is an awe-ful scientist. During his decades as a jet pilot, he also turned his very scientific mind to tending and observing bees. In Peru's Sacred Valley, he is working to increase the number of bees and to educate others about their importance. Jerry turns the reductive eye of his mind to the bees with absolutely no presumption that their obvious intelligence is less than the intelligence of the whole within which they operate, or less than human intelligence. It is apparent to him that the bees are a window into the greater intelligence of which they are a part.

Jerry's objective in working with the bees is not to maximize the production of honey, as is the case with many producers. Rather, he is interested in how the work of the bees can be supported by his connection, communication, and collaboration with them. In the process, he discovers how much support bees provide to the earth and to humans, and he discovers new ways of providing support to them.

Tribes have to bring awe-ful science into the creation of their tambos. We need to look to the wisdom of our ancestors not as a way of finding our way back, but of finding our way forward. We need to learn to connect, commune, and collaborate with all elements of the earth in order to co-evolve with the earth, just as we have the capacity and need to co-evolve with bees. Tambos can represent a practical application of that principle.

Working with bees, water quality and supply, crop diversity and resilience, soil health, and alternatives to fossil fuels are examples of a far greater spectrum of activities in which a tambo must engage to become an intentional and conscious part of the ecology upon which it is dependent. Successful soul-tribing will require the best of awe-ful science.

A Collaborative Team

I imagine at least eight members or groups within the tribe that function in a form of synergetic collaboration. By numbering them, I don't mean to imply a hierarchy of relative importance, nor that there couldn't be more or fewer groups.

The first are the elders.

The second are people who are native to the area within which the tambo is to be located—people who have the knowledge of how to grow food and tend animals, as well as a deeper knowledge of the communities and culture in which the tambo is located. This latter group would be, like the elders, longer-term members of the tribe. They would be invited not only because of the necessary connection of a tribe to its surrounding communities, but for their practical knowledge and their interest in working in service to the vision and mission of the tribe. Like the elders, these people may have families with children of all ages who support the life of the tambo by their presence and who are supported by the tambo in an expression of ayni.

The third and fourth groups would be those souls that it is the tambo's mission to support. Both of these groups would consist of those people who resonate with the tribal vision and mission and come for the experience that the tribe and tambo offer.

The difference between the third and fourth groups is simply one of time. One group will come for a shorter time. That group might compensate the tribe with money, although the relationship with money is one that the tribe needs to examine. The other group will spend more time, perhaps exchanging labor for the experience. There may be other modalities of exchange. A short time might be two to three weeks; a longer time, two or more months. Souls working at Stage Three, Four and Five might be in either of these two groups.

The fifth group would include shamans, curanderos, pacos, teachers, and other facilitators who have a special skill to contribute. Members of this group might stay for longer times or they may be visitors. An elder at one center might fall into this fifth group in another center, as these tribal communities network in service of the support of their members.

There is a sixth group, already mentioned, that must be included. Each tambo will garner a group of angels, guides, ancestral spirits, plant spirits, and archetypal spirits that are also devoted to this work of soul support. As tambos emerge, representatives of these fields of intelligence will present themselves and await recognition so that they can be of service. No tambo could be complete without the spirits who support the teaching and protect the place. And such spirits, like people, come and go as well.

Seventh, the place itself can be an active member of this synergetic gathering.

Last, there are the other "people" who often fade into our largely invisible environment. These are the stone people, the green and growing people, the creepy crawlers, and the furred, finned, and flying people. Like humans, they each and all participate in an ecology operating within an infinite field of intelligence vaster than any of its parts. The job of the tambos is to discover how to connect, commune, collaborate, and co-evolve with that intelligence not only directly but through each of its manifestations. Humans will not otherwise survive to do their work of consciousness.

Within this group is a special category of master teaching plants to which I want to give particular attention.

The Plants

In Peru, the master teaching plants are ayahuasca, huachuma, and tobacco. Although working with these plants is an optional aspect of tambos, I want to include considerations relative to the option of an ongoing relationship with these plants and the fields of intelligence that lie behind them.

Like relationships of any kind, the relationship with these medicine plants and the fields of intelligence to which they provide access is one that must be cultivated with practice, patience, and respect. And as with all other relationships, this one must also be held in ayni, by which the tribe takes responsibility for its role in its use of the plants and reciprocates for the gifts that the plants bring.

As I have suggested in a prior chapter, these plants are not for all souls at all times. I never recommend to people that they use these plants, and don't intend to imply such a recommendation in proposing a vision of soul tribes and tambos. On the contrary, I suggest that people not engage them if they are not ready to take responsibility for developing the skills necessary to meet the plants and integrate the changes that the plants may facilitate.

Some souls at particular stages of their own explorations may benefit from working with these powerful plants when guided by people who are capable of guiding this encounter. These plants work from a frame of mysterious intelligence that the human mind will not likely penetrate with an understanding equal to the heart's ability to connect to it. No dogma will attach to them. It is important always to ask the plants for their direction in how a particular soul can best engage them. This, finally, is the responsibility of the tribal elders.

Food

I am unaware of any encounter with the plant medicines in which the facilitator did not have some opinion about how a participant should eat, or not eat, before drinking the medicine. What has interested me is that the instructions are not particularly consistent, and how many of the beliefs seem to be based on rumor.

An authoritative source might be a long-experienced shaman, but it is certainly not the American owner of an Iquitos restaurant, to whom is occasionally attributed the infamous ayahuasca diet. I've been told that the bland diet that is often suggested as the best preparation for the ayahuasca is simply local comfort food that has no particular implication for taking the medicine. Although most of the advice I've heard tends toward eating less in preparation for the plant encounter, my experience has in some degree suggested otherwise.

This question remains inadequately researched and would be an interesting subject for exploration in the setting of a tambo that is working with the plant medicines as a central part of its program. But there is quite another reason to be concerned with food.

My primary concern is the question of how to best support the body in general with food that can be grown in the area of the tambo. A program designed to coax the body into a posture of providing the optimal vehicle for the soul's work must attend to the optimal health of the body. Every tambo needs to have a conscious approach to growing, preparing, and eating the food that is best for the body and its ability to work in an energetically harmonic way with the subtle energies that soul work requires. Because bodies are different and have varying needs, I feel that dietary dogma and narrow dietary plans are not the best companions for this work.

Tambos need to be familiar with the nutritional, medicinal, and spiritual nature of the plants in the places where they are located. This is a primary reason that local people who are knowledgeable with the area need to be a part of the tambo's work. This is part of the knowledge base that tambos need to understand, serve, and protect.

When we deepen our relationship with the earth, we need to open our minds to see how the earth has been so beautifully designed in so many ways to support the viability of the human body that in turn supports the human enterprise in general. This is a primary concern of the business of tambos, and food is one doorway through which that exploration can occur.

Research

I suspect that divine curiosity began the process of which souls are agents. Souls are in the business of expanding consciousness in service of the process of creating.

The soul tribe is an amplification of this soul nature. Its very presence is an exercise in courting the unknown and learning how to engage it. Underlying all of what the tribe does is an attitude of interest, curiosity, and humility about how little we know. If we can connect, we can commune in order to communicate as a means of creating the collaboration that serves co-creation of the cosmos.

Balancing Specialization with Generalization

The postmodern world is one of specialization. While specialization offers a certain benefit by dividing labor and deepening discrete skills and information sets, it also offers narrow viewpoints and the opportunity to avoid responsibility for the complex human role in the ecology of the planet. Culture's recent race to specialization and its narrow views have contributed significantly to the mess in which we find ourselves.

As a small-town lawyer representing some corporate clients with diverse interests and large resources, it was necessary for me to be a generalist in my work. It was also necessary for me to hire specialists to work on particular client issues.

I found that the specialists I hired could seldom get the bigger view and that leaving solutions to them alone caused other problems. I had to learn to listen to them and incorporate their knowledge without deferring responsibility for decision-making to them. I had to hold the bigger view. Because specialists had become the power players in the legal world, it was not easy for me not to defer.

A tambo has to be, in its collective, a generalist in the work of living on the earth. It has to learn to do everything, as farmers not so long ago had to learn to do everything. There is no benefit in America's specialization of its agricultural resources in corn and soybeans, when the narrow focus prevents us from recognizing the damage done by our mono-cultural practices, which include overuse of corn and soy in prepared foods, use of pesticides, and unwise misallocation of water. There is, however, value in the opportunity a specialist has to look deeply into what the scientific eye can see. But, at the same time, we need to achieve and hold a global, holistic view.

Within any tambo, there must be those who can hold the broad view and those who can achieve a deep view. We need to operate stereoscopically, using mind and heart simultaneously.

Grounding

Perhaps nothing accelerates the evolution of human consciousness more than the soul's work in collaboration with the body. Our larger tribes of origin do not consciously support this work, and souls need to create alternative models that do.

Grounding is the nature of soul work. Without the body, the soul has no traction upon the earth to further heaven's purpose. Like an extraordinarily complex computer, the body is hardware to software that is the soul—one is of little good without the other.

Without the soul's unique capacity to download heaven's continually updating software, the body has no purpose to fulfill with its physical power, nor intelligence sufficient to sustain itself upon the earth. This work is about coming to ground, learning to ground, using the ground, and grounding in ways deeper than we have imagined before.

II

A SOUL HOME OF THE HEART

IN PERU, IT IS EASY TO SEE the opportunity for bringing a new consciousness to the process of creating community for emerging souls. For me, that new consciousness is a soul perspective and the depth of skill and experience that it represents.

It takes no deep discernment to see that humans are at a critical juncture and that new strategies for living on this planet need to emerge now. Some deeper discernment will sense the urgency the helper beings from other dimensions are conveying to us. They speak directly to our souls, and they are encouraging us to bring our souls out of their sleepy enmeshment with the body and its personality. Combining the soul perspective with purposeful tribes and tambos in full communication with heaven and earth is a way of responding to that sense of urgency for those of us who are also feeling it in our hearts, bodies, and souls.

Postmodern prosperity and technology have created an opportunity for large numbers of individuals to break from their tribes of origin and move about the whole of the world to stimulate the emergence of their destinies. This window of opportunity creates a possibility of the proliferation of the small, breakaway tribes that support this soul evolution.

This view is not to diminish the importance of the work of the souls who choose to stay in the tribes of origin for the purpose of evolving themselves or those tribes. It is instead to say that there is another form of work that other souls are being called to do and that tambos offer support for all of this soul work.

As time and experience have passed in my life, it has become easy for me to think of consciousness as love. But it is another matter altogether for soul-as-love to transform the world of matter into an expression of that love. As we develop increasing skills of heart-based attention, we can begin to learn how to better love ourselves, to discover our own destinies, to skillfully love others, and to participate in the infinity of creative ways to express love in forming time/space anew. From a soul perspective, there is no deeper work than learning how to love and how to put that love to work. This exploration is the evolutionary work of tribes and tambos.

Soul evolution arises in the space of the heart. Through the heart, the focused consciousness we know as attention can return to its immediate source, which is the soul itself. Through the portal of the heart, the soul can begin its inter-dimensional work of courting and enlisting the body into the work of courting matter itself into new forms.

With these understandings, souls can gather in special places, leave from time to time in order to continue their work of destiny, and re-gather in these homes away from their work of the moment. They can gather in tambos that are the home of the heart for souls burning with love.

Skillful souls breathe the inspirations of heaven into the body, and breathe new creation out. As the ayahuasca whispered to me in ceremony, *don't waste your breath.* Breath literally connects soul to body and underwrites our ability to create. Your ability to create is far too precious to waste, and it is not for you alone. You are part of what is happening in a cosmic space that is beyond what any of our minds can fully comprehend, and the pace is picking up.

Come when your heart calls your soul to its new home. Someone will be waiting here for you.

AN AFTERWORD FROM GRACE

AS THE WORK on this book was coming to a close, I spoke with Grace, whom you met in Chapter Two. I asked her to reflect upon the years that have passed since we first met. Although some of the sentiments she expresses here do not coincide with my own, what she sent to me felt like a clear, lived experience of a part of what I have attempted to convey in this book and in The Soul's Critical Path.

A year after my accident, I met John. He introduced me to a healing modality for my still unrecovered head injury. From the moment of that first heart-based soul retrieval, the journey to heal my life also began. And the first step was indeed getting out of my head so I could start to deal with how I felt. It was during this time that the world started coming into focus: not how it "should" be, but how it really is.

My accident left me with impaired brain filters which allowed my highly empathic nature to come to the forefront. I realized that I could not only feel what people around me were feeling, but that I could also feel the earth in a far more direct way than before. And I felt that She was full of sorrow.

The early days of my new work with myself were hallmarked by this sorrow. I now understand that my body resonated with a planet that has been treated as a limitless and boundless resource instead of a finite being, in the same way women in this culture are treated.

We were the same, the earth and I. Neither of us could impose dearly needed boundaries, yet we were both full of sorrow that so much was being taken from us, full of sorrow at our seeming inability to stop giving too much. From this identification with the earth came the experience of connection as well. I was not alone. From this sense of connection grew the next stage of my life.

A year into my work with John, I moved from Colorado to Washington to be with friends who'd recently relocated to start an organic farm. Having just broken up with my boyfriend and on rocky terms with most of my biological family, I sunk my hands into the dirt and grounded into my new home.

This initial quest for land and tribe failed as it was connected to agriculture, which we would later discover to be another means of creating separation rather than connection. But we were working without a map, striving to create something we had not experienced before. Mistakes and missteps have been simply part of finding the path hidden under all this concrete.

Despite seeming failures upon the way, the core of our group has stuck together. We always joked that only those of us who could deal with our "shit" stayed. Somehow we agreed to evolve together and to evolve our definition of tribe.

The experience of farming helped me to launch into the world with my first trip to Peru. Something about working with the soil strengthened my resolve. Even though I was still tortured by fear and self-doubt, I pushed through it. My journey was guided from the beginning, and I was able to navigate dangerous situations. Every need I had was cared for, save one—the big one—the one that defines my path as different from many others in this spiritual world. I had been socialized to such an extent that I had accepted the socialized identity as my own.

I had been taught to deny my inner self. Despite having a new courage to move forward, something deep inside me still believed that my new direction was wrong and going against the proper way to live. I sensed that I had been socialized to believe that whatever I felt deep within was wrong. Yet, alongside that feeling was an urge that propelled me forward, an urge to belong. Now, I could see how this deep desire to belong springs from a need for tribe, even as it was initially propelled by a sense of low self-worth. I thought that, if I could just belong somewhere, if I could just be accepted and seen, I could prove I wasn't bad. What I got instead of a sense of belonging and safety was a walk through the underworld, a dance with shadow.

Instead of getting easier, my journey got much harder. For several years after the first Peru trip, I was confronted with many challenges, each one forcing me to delve further and further into the source of my motivations and reactions. From unsuccessful romantic relationships to losing friends, from homelessness and joblessness, to nine months of fibroid hemorrhaging, Spirit forced me to face my shadow time and time again.

Through all that I did achieve at this time, I never achieved a sense of safety or belonging. I returned to Peru, doing more plant medicine work than during my first trip. I continued to struggle with anger and antibiotic-resistant giardia.

A notable change took place during this trip. I realized without a doubt that I was homesick for my home in the United States, not for a house or a person or a food, but for the land, for the blue-grey mountains laced with morning mist, for the fingers of land jutting out into slate grey Puget Sound waters, for the call of the blue Heron, for the myriad kinds of rain, and for the sweet touch of the sun poking through the clouds on a spring afternoon. Without a doubt, I was in love with the land of my country. My country. My land. My love. I no longer wanted to run away. This beauty, this being was worth fighting for. So, with no money and completely physically debilitated, I went home.

Back in the States, I discovered that I had changed, but the world had not. It became clear that I would need more than passion. I would need money. I accepted a position processing fish on a large boat in the Bering Sea, grading roe at sea for 100 hours a week. I knew I could do this. Just ten short weeks, and I could be headed with full pockets to a dream year of farming and traveling.

Despite my experience with hardship, I was utterly unprepared for this experience. What I thought would be a short trip soon turned into my own personal hell that continued to push me to the breaking point. I experienced walking pneumonia, a separated shoulder joint, and sexual harassment. These were just the tip of the iceberg. My inner critic was on full volume.

I continued to beat myself up until the night a man came into my room and demanded sex. I solved the problem with the help of my roommate and a large rock that I slept with. It took me two weeks to gather the courage to tell the captain what was happening, during which time this man continued to harass me mercilessly. In the end it was tell or risk being seriously hurt.

This was the turning point. I'd never been taught to have boundaries, or that I deserved them, or really even what they were. I had to be pushed to my absolute breaking point.

Now, I fought back. I screamed and raised hell until the captain took me seriously. Once I claimed my power in the situation and really had his attention, I was able to dictate what I needed and how that looked. That was absolutely unheard of on a boat of this kind.

For the first time I was able to really put what society had made me believe about myself to the side. I was able to put my ego and emotions aside. I was able to see myself less as a tortured soul fucking up her life and more as a soul in school. The hard lessons of this life came into view, and I became aware that they were designed to bring me up to speed very quickly in this lifetime so that I might do the work of my soul on this planet in this time.

With this experience, I've been able to move forward into integrating the lessons, to sink into that soul knowing, to strip back the layers of the old self, and to let my own inner compass take control. I've danced two Narayas (a Shoshone round dance for healing), taken classes that have helped me learn how to sink into joy and bliss, and begun to sink into the intuitive and spontaneous nature of my own magic. I'm beginning to learn how to stand fully in my power. Maybe I still don't see the full picture, but it's coming into view. My tribe, now grown and changed, continues to share that vision with me.

Although my immediate and most personal tribe consists of about six people, our tribe at large is much bigger. Thousands of folks mostly from the West Coast and others from around the country compose our larger tribe. These people have many different takes on the world and how they carry spirit into it. Far from being a disadvantage, though, this allows for growth and movement all within the larger spiritual tribe.

Instead of leaving each other when our needs have changed, smaller groups within the larger tribe shift in order to account for individual changes. Thus, we never leave our tribe, but rather have the space to grow and change within it. It's a constant reshuffling, and it's so amazing. Although we don't share the exact same beliefs, we do know that we are closer in heart and mind than we are to the dominant culture.

Although my tribe is in Oregon, I can travel to Seattle, Santa Cruz, the Bay Area, and many other places where I can be welcomed by my tribe.

The tribe has moved away from farming, for it became clear along the way that it was agriculture that led us away from the land in the first place and only held us separate and apart from the world. We have moved toward what we call bioregional animism, or place-based magic. We have the collective vision of re-wilding people and place and dismantling dominant culture as we know it.

We want collapse. We're pushing for it. In many ways I think to soften or reverse it would be doing ourselves and the world at large a great disservice. Many of us feel our work is to help push America over the edge. The channeled piece that comes as I write this is "it is the only way to break or reverse the lie of separation."

We aspire to living a life informed by the land instead of one that we impose upon the land, as does the culture of agri-culture.

We know that all we can hope for in this lifetime is to become feral and to plant seeds for the future, even as we understand that we will never be wild in the way that our indigenous souls crave.

We know humans have been so socialized that they've forgotten their wild roots. It is not just about what we will discover for ourselves. We are just the bridge, and we may never see the change that arises from our seeding. Perhaps we can give others a life devoid of this lie that we are separate and alone. I do know that we can't go back to the days before the damage was done, and that we can't continue forward on this trajectory of civilization.

I also believe that spirit doesn't make mistakes. There's something important in the mess we've made of the world and ourselves, and it's our job to perform the alchemy of combining the old ways with the new to create something that has not existed before. It's our job to write the new mythology so that we might all walk into a new world.

When we love both the parts that seemed bad and those that seemed good, when we move spirit into matter, they become a wholly new being. I know now without a doubt that I will never fit in with society. I'm not supposed to. I will never belong or feel at home in the socialized world. As hard and painful as that perspective has been for me, I know now that my embrace of that feeling is one of the biggest gifts I can give the world.

So I say to society, I don't fit into your mold, and neither do you. Forge your own way, move forward with your own compass, live with your own love, and manifest your own magic.

APPENDIX

An Overview of the Parts and Stages from
The Soul's Critical Path: Waking Down to the Soul's Purpose, the Body's Power, and the Heart's Passion

My own experience suggested to me that the terrain over which the soul's trajectory travels might be sensibly divided into six parts, along with six corresponding stages of consciousness that are roughly associated with those parts. These six parts and stages constitute what I have called the critical path of the soul.

1. PART ONE / STAGE ONE

Terrain of the Soul Journey	Stage of Consciousness	Perspective
Part One: The gathering place of souls intermediate between heaven and earth	Stage One: The soul knows that it is a soul and consciously, if not skillfully, knows that it is called upon to choose another round on the planet.	The earth journey is the soul's opportunity to learn.

The terrain that is Part One of the soul journey is the "place" described by Er as the meadow.

In this gathering place, the nature of the soul's consciousness is that it knows itself to be a soul seeing directly through its own eyes. This is a soul perspective. Although a self-aware soul perspective, it is not necessarily a developed or mature perspective. Whatever the level of development, this is Stage One Consciousness.

In that self-aware state, the soul chooses a life. The Sisters imprint a fate upon that life—a fate that is not disclosed. The soul drinks from the River of Forgetting. The soul is swept away to be born upon the earth, carrying a secret that it will keep even from itself until the skillful means of discovery of that secret has been acquired. The secret is that soul's destiny and how that destiny is embedded in the soul's fate.

2. PART TWO / STAGE TWO

Terrain of the Soul Journey	Stage of Consciousness	Perspective
Part Two: The dense body field and the earth	Stage Two: Attention is captured by the body, held in a provisional personality, and entrained outward by culture. The soul has lost control of the ability to control its own attention.	Life is a struggle. I (the personality) am a victim of circumstances. Things that happen to me are either good or bad. The bad is my fate. I can't control my fate or emotional reactions because those depend on what happens to me. Life is out of my control unless I outsmart it.

Part Two of the terrain of the soul's trajectory is the body. Coming to the earth for the birth of the body represents the beginning, but not the end, of a process of merger. That merger first involves a mutual entrainment of the respective fields of the body and the soul to a degree sufficient to sustain life in the body. The further progress of this entrainment is not automatic. The initial stages of this entrainment are unconscious to the soul. Further entrainment requires skillful attention, which represents the work of the ensuing stages of consciousness at the soul level. If the soul experiences the body to be alien territory, that's because it is. And the body, similarly, may experience the soul as an invader.

This second stage of consciousness is characterized by the inability of the soul to control attention, thereby defaulting attention to culture's control of an immature personality—a default personality that reflects the stronger identification with the body, an attention directed outward, and an almost total absence of awareness of the soul. Modern culture takes advantage of that opportunity intentionally, mercilessly, and skillfully. In this environment, particularly without the presence of a nurturing connection with the earth, the surface personality often feels out of control. For the personality that arises from this preliminary merger of soul and body in a challenging environment, this is the stage of victim mentality and an engagement with the external world that excludes the inner. Dissociation, depression, and a deeply felt sense of disconnection are common as the personality finds itself unable to make sense of the world or navigate skillfully in it.

3. STAGE THREE / PART THREE

Terrain of the Soul Journey	Stage of Consciousness	Perspective
Part Three: The terrain includes the body, but also includes the other dimensions apart beyond time/space. There is a move from the exclusively external to include the internal.	Stage Three: A battle for control of attention begins, with culture on one side, and the nascent soul on the other. The soul is now working, even below the level of conscious awareness, to capture control of the attention that has been taken by the personality and culture during the soul's forgetfulness.	Life remains confusing even as a sense of purpose has begun to form. I begin to shift from seeing everything as good or bad, to seeing what happens as *just is*. Reactivity begins to diminish as I learn to reclaim the projections that are the basis of my victim perspective.

Part Three of the terrain has now expanded in the same way that the soul's awareness has also begun to expand. The soul is aware not only of the density of its body but also of the heaven dimensions that call out to it, helping the soul to awaken and emerge. We may feel these as awakenings—stirrings, intuitions, knowings, and peak "spiritual" experiences.

Within Stage Three Consciousness, small awakenings may occur many times until they form the critical mass sufficient to shift from a personality perspective that excludes the soul to one that begins to contemplate the presence of the soul. Even though the ultimate work of the soul involves a full partnership with the body, with attention in the control of the soul, this preliminary part of the soul work is about remembering itself. This step carries the attention back away from the body—including its thoughts, feelings, and sensory attachments—to a remembrance of the fundamental sense of connection that is the mature soul's natural state.

Like my own near-death experience, there is a return to a consciousness of the heaven dimensions. For some religions, that return would be the end of the journey and possibly—from some perspectives—the end of a punishment that the earth journey has represented. But from the soul perspective that I am suggesting here, this gradual return to awareness of the heaven dimensions and the increasing access to "peak" experiences are only a preparation for the next stage. Stage Three Consciousness is about recognizing something we've known, but from a much different perspective. In that remembrance, we know heaven for the first time from the soul's perspective of being in the body. We begin to acquaint ourselves with the body from the perspective of the soul's connection to heaven. Remembering that we are souls that left heaven allows us to get to work on the question of why we left that place and came to the earth journey to work in an unfamiliar body. This remembrance may occur in a dramatic manner, as occurred for me with the near-death experience, or in the variety of ways we will discover as we begin to focus on achieving a soul perspective. With this remembrance restored firmly in the soul's consciousness, the soul is ready to move forward to the deeper work of embodiment.

In short, Stage Three Consciousness involves the process of learning how to control attention, learning how to wrest it from the grasp of the body and culture, placing that attention in the heart-field where the soul's awareness of itself is cultivated, and ultimately shifting identity from the personality to the soul.

4. PART FOUR / STAGE FOUR

Terrain of the Soul Journey	Stage of Consciousness	Perspective
Part Four: Anywhere that the empowered soul now directs its attention, including the body field, the other dimensions, or the soul itself.	Stage Four: The soul has now captured control of attention and is able to direct attention, with some effort, to itself, to the body, and to other dimensions that contain information for the soul's further journey, setting the stage for learning how to engage more deeply with each of those destinations.	Life and its challenges are neither good nor bad, nor "just is." Life's challenges are now a gift of opportunity for soul development. "I" is now characterized increasingly by my identification with soul rather than with the personality. The soul now assumes responsibility for creating a partnership with the body in the service of the emergence of soul destiny. I no longer project responsibility for my fate or destiny on everything and everyone else. I am no longer a victim.

The peak experiences encountered during Stage Three Consciousness now provide meaning for our day-to-day experience of life in Part Four of the journey. While the terrain of Part Three and Part Four is the same, our experience with it becomes more intentional, intense, and skillful during Stage Four Consciousness. My landing onto the runway of my body was a second landing within the same lifetime—a second coming of the soul in a moment of awakening that begins a purposeful effort by the soul to partner with the body in service of soul's work.

This fourth part of the trajectory is less familiar in our culture, or in any culture for that matter. Aurobindo made it his life's work to talk about its beginning and its potential for bringing consciousness to the very cells of the body, even as he acknowledged that he did not accomplish it. This is the stage to which the notion of Tantric practice—*Vajrayana*—is introduced even though its potential is explored only in Stage Five. In Stage Four Consciousness, we begin to use the soul's growing control over attention to discover and engage the variety of dimensions of reality, including the fields of body, earth, heaven, fate, destiny, and the soul itself. Stage Four also represents a looking back upon the prior stages as we identify and resolve the dysfunctional patterns that have blocked the soul's emergence. So Stage Four represents the time of healing the body-based consequences of a victim perspective and developing the skills of soul attention, both of which are necessary to power the soul toward its destiny.

5. PART FIVE / STAGE FIVE

Terrain of the Soul Journey	Stage of Consciousness	Perspective
Part Five: The body is now the temporary home base of the soul as it explores the density of time/space in the context of its connection with the other-dimensional fields that provide constant support for the soul journey.	Stage Five: The soul's ability to focus attention grows as it goes increasingly into the other dimensions, and as it explores the density of matter. The soul's control of attention is no longer simply conscious and intentional, but increasingly automatic and therefore, one might say, becoming more *skilled*.	Life is often joyful and full of energy, yet even more challenging in new ways. The soul's work is at the edge of the evolution of consciousness through the expression of its own purpose through the power of the body and the passion of the heart. I identify both with the whole of consciousness and with my particular soul role as a co-creator of the play of consciousness.

The terrain remains cosmic, including every possible field that soul consciousness can visit, but the focus is upon deepening the soul's relationship with the body and earth, which is the frontier of human consciousness. We have called the stage that follows death the frontier, but that is only because we have failed to see the frontier which lies more immediately before us in this lifetime. The death stage is well traveled, but the exploration of the body/earth fields by a soul fully grounded in the heart with skillful control of attention is the very definition of the frontier of human consciousness. This is the exploration that we have come to do. We cannot leapfrog over the earlier stages and start our work here. We must all pay our dues and gain admission to Stage Five by working through the prior stages.

6. PART SIX / STAGE SIX

Terrain of the Soul Journey	Stage of Consciousness	Perspective
Part Six: The bridge between body and the heaven dimensions that forms upon the death of the body	Stage Six: If the soul has managed to control attention, then this is a direct and smooth transition. If the soul remains in Stage Two or Three Consciousness, the transition is more complex because of the personality's confusion about the process of death.	Death is a transition back to a self-aware soul state, although that remembrance may not occur immediately, and a soul confusion that occurs during life may persist for some time beyond death.

Part Six terrain is the short bridge to the heaven dimensions, to which we journey upon death without prospect of return to this body. Stage Six Consciousness is a wide-awake approach to the transition of dying. All of our preparation for this transition occurs in earlier stages of consciousness as the skill of attention and the experience of using it develop and mature. That maturation may define our ability to focus attention into the death transition itself. Without that preparation, a transition from body to the heaven dimensions will occur, but it may occur in the midst of an earlier stage of consciousness. Many people experience this transition from a consciousness that is characterized by Stage Two Consciousness, a lucky few in Stage Three, fewer in Stage Four, and a smaller number in Stage Five. I suspect, from my reading and the felt sense that is emerging in me, that coming to Stage Six from Stage Five may present other opportunities, but that is beyond the scope of this book.

A Visual Schematic of the Soul Journey

In short, the potential of this journey is that we jump "down" from heaven, hopefully recover from the fall, do the work of waking up by which we find our way "upward" to the experience that refreshes the memory that we came from heaven on purpose, do some wide-ranging healing and practice with our newly growing soul consciousness, then focus that awakening consciousness back down into the body and the density of matter as far as we can with the help of the other-dimensional fields (frequency encoded with information), all before the soul leaves the body and returns to heaven—a down, then an up, then another down before the last up when the body dies. A picture of that trajectory might look like this (the numbers refer to the six stages of consciousness):

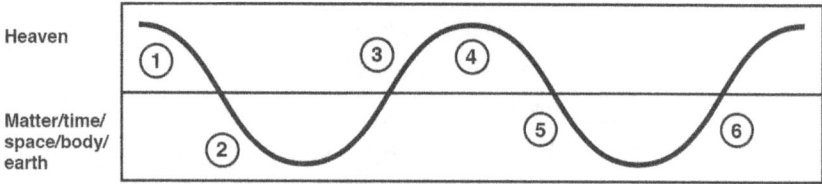

Associating labels with a line drawing doesn't give you a meaningful experience. Nevertheless, these conceptual tools help to organize what is otherwise chaotic and constantly moving information into a framework that may be helpful until your own internal territory is familiar and your movement within it becomes increasingly intuitive. The linear map helps a linear mind—and we need that linear mind even if it's a mistake to let it rule our lives—to chart some progress over longer time frames than a moment or a day. More importantly, it may help the linear mind open to a partnership with the soul through the heart.

Although it may be helpful to have a kind of rough visual of this up-and-down process divided into parts and stages, such a schematic is far too simplistic and linear to be an accurate representation of the progression of the soul in a day-to-day way. It is, after all, only a map; it is not the territory. And even though the map shows an idealized trajectory in the form of a critical path, we sometimes stand still, hesitate, go backwards, or sideways, and forget what we are up to. Even if I am living mostly in Stage Four, I may spend a particularly difficult week in Stage Two until my partner reminds me that I have regressed.

None of us is completely in Part Two/Stage Two to the exclusion of Part Three/ Stage Three. Within each stage, there is a beginning, middle, and emergence into the beginning of the next. When I speak of being in one stage or another, it is really more accurate to say that the stage represents the nature of challenges with which our consciousness is faced at a particular time. To say that we are in a particular stage of consciousness is simply to say that a particular form of identity and relationship with attention is a predominant, though not exclusive, state of consciousness at a particular point in time. We routinely go back and forth between stages in particular moments, but the trend—if we persist—is to move in an arc that has identifiable benchmarks, such as the parts and stages that I am identifying here.

The signs I'm posting along the way—*parts* and *stages*—are ways of marking the milestones on the journey by saying "this is different than that," "there's a direction to the journey," and "there's a purpose embedded in this experience." Noting milestones allows us to mark a position or sense a movement and understand that something a little different is significant even if it is subtle. If we were talking about a roadmap laid out on the geography of the earth, it would be easier to see. It's more challenging to talk about consciousness. The tools are metaphor and similes, feelings, experiences, knowings, and partial understandings that we abandon when we get better understandings—much tougher territory to navigate than learning math or driving the Interstate.

Our ultimate spiritual work on this journey is to get soul consciousness into the body and become the agents of consciousness through which heaven collaborates with earth to co-create at the edge of the evolution of consciousness itself. The challenge is not merely to experience consciousness beyond the body in the heaven dimensions, but to bring it into the body and to experience it fully there—here, now. No one knows where that process will lead. That is both its delight and challenge. There may be spiritual work beyond this journey, but we probably won't know what that is until we have lived this one out.

www.ingramcontent.com/pod-product-compliance
Lightning Source LLC
Chambersburg PA
CBHW051758040426
42446CB00007B/427